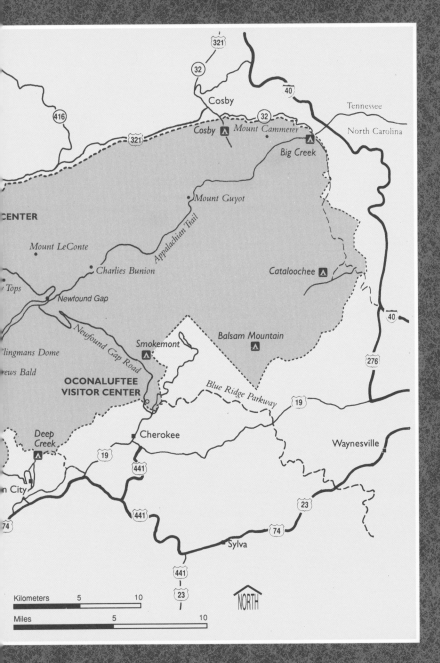

GREAT
SMOKY
MOUNTAINS

Connie Toops

VOYAGEUR PRESS

The author gratefully acknowledges the assistance of Keith Langdon, Bob and Pat Momich, Kermit and Lois Caughron, Pat Toops, and editor Elizabeth Knight in the preparation of this book.

Printed in Hong Kong
92   93   94   95   96   5   4   3   2   1

Library of Congress Cataloging-in-Publication Data
Toops, Connie M.
    Great smoky mountains / Connie Toops.
        p.   cm.
    ISBN 0-89658-162-4
        1. Great Smoky Mountains (N.C. and Tenn.)   2. Great Smoky
Mountains National Park (N.C. and Tenn.)   I. Title.
F443.G7T66   1992
976.8'89—dc20
                                                                91-39958
                                                                CIP

Published by
Voyageur Press, Inc.
P.O. Box 338, 123 North Second Street
Stillwater, MN 55082 U.S.A.
From Minnesota and Canada 612-430-2210
Toll-free 800-888-9653

Voyageur Press books are also available at discounts for quantities for educational, fundraising, premium, or sales-promotion use. For details contact the marketing department. Please write or call for our free catalog of natural history publications.

CONTENTS

SMOKIES SUPERLATIVES

The Great Smoky Mountains are the crown jewels of the Appalachians. For nearly sixty miles along the Tennessee-North Carolina border, an imposing phalanx of broad-shouldered peaks rises into the clouds. Expansive views from Smokies summits are framed by stark rock outcrops and windswept trees. Below, emerald valleys lie in a serene and densely forested contrast. They host abundant wildlife—from deer prancing in the fog and black bears teaching their cubs the ways of the woods to minute members of the forest community hidden under leaves and logs. In spring and summer, the mountains are covered with cascades of wildflowers. Fall's glorious finale transforms them into a brief mardi gras of colors and dazzling light before the somber months of winter return.

Earliest descriptions of these southern Appalachians called the highlands the "Cherokee Mountains" in reference to Native Americans who lived here. Cherokees knew the region as *Shaconage*, "mountains of the blue smoke." Not until 1789 were the names "Great Iron" and "Great Smoaky" mentioned. This reference to "smoke" describes the blue-gray haze that frequently envelops the mountains. The haze results, in part, from transpiration of moisture by trees, shrubs, and herbaceous plants.

In 1926 an 812-square-mile area within the heart of this region received congressional approval to become Great Smoky Mountains National Park. With elevations ranging from about a thousand feet above sea level at Happy Valley, on the park's western boundary, to Clingmans Dome, Mount LeConte, and Mount Guyot, all over 6,500 feet, the flora and fauna here are so diverse that the Great Smokies have been recognized as an International Biosphere Reserve.

This status is enumerated in a litany of superlatives. Within a space sixteen miles wide by fifty miles long, Great Smoky Mountains National Park is home to 1,535 species of flowering plants. Counted among these are 135 types of trees and large shrubs, more variety than in all of Europe! About twenty outstanding specimens in the park are the largest trees of their kind. They include a tulip poplar in Albright Cove twenty-four feet in circumference, a cucumber magnolia near Greenbrier that measures eighteen feet around, and a gnarled yellow buckeye on the north side of Maddron Bald whose girth of sixteen feet requires three adults joining hands to circle its base.

Seventy-one kinds of mammals have been recorded in the park, along with 236 species of birds, thirty-five types of reptiles, and forty-six varieties of fish—more than in the fresh water of any other park in the nation. Twenty-two species of salamanders dwell here, a number greater than in any similar-sized region of the world. This is a place were scientists are still questing for knowledge. Within the past few years, dragonflies, shield ferns, and fen orchids new to the park have been identified.

Like a sparkling gemstone, Great Smoky Mountains National Park has many facets. In addition to its varied plants and animals, pristine streams, and breathtaking mountain vistas, the park is a living museum of the folklife of mountain pioneers.

The Great Smoky Mountains rise for nearly sixty miles along the Tennessee–North Carolina border. The Smokies are known as the "crown jewels" of the Appalachian mountain chain because of their diverse plant and animal life.

Not surprisingly, since the Great Smokies lie within a two-day drive of virtually every resident in the eastern United States, this is the most-visited national park in the country. In a typical year, eight to nine million people tour the park, with nearly a fourth of them arriving during the month of prime autumn color.

Yet for those seeking solitude, three-quarters of the park is wilderness. Most visitors remain on paved roads and a few favorite trails. With more than nine hundred miles of hiking paths and a hundred miles of gravel byways, there are always places to leave the clamor of the crowd for the isolation of the forest.

It is deep within these coves and hollows that the Smokies work their magic. On unhurried walks, glimpses of new fawns among the dappled shadows or discoveries of fragile orchids emerging from the leaf litter restore our inner peace. In the Great Smokies, seekers of wilderness find insight into themselves as well as into the wonders of these ancient mountains.

Black-throated green warblers migrate from their winter homes in Central America to nest in the Great Smokies. They are among the 236 species of birds recorded within the park. (Photo © by Maslowski Wildlife Productions)

Above: *Lush valleys are home to abundant wildlife including deer that prance in the morning fog at Cades Cove.* **Left:** *Pink lady's slipper orchids.* **Right:** *Great Smoky Mountains National Park is a living museum of the mountain pioneer, preserving cabins, barns, schools, and churches in former settlements such as Cades Cove, Cataloochee, and Oconaluftee.*

FROM ROCKY CRAGS TO FERTILE COVES

Standing on a grand promontory in the Smokies and gazing out toward a distant summit, you sense these are old mountains. Unlike the raw-boned, jagged peaks of the Cascades and Sierras in the American West—shapes that imply the earth-shaking violence of recent formation—the Great Smokies have a stooped and rounded outline.

The Appalachian Mountains, of which the Great Smokies are one of many components, span 1,500 miles, arching northeast from Alabama and Georgia in the United States into Canada. Although the range may have once been as high as the Rocky Mountains, only the backbones of Appalachian giants remain. The highest is 6,684-foot Mount Mitchell in North Carolina's Black Mountains. The Appalachians reach their widest expanse in Tennessee and North Carolina. Here the Smokies form a broad rampart amid neighboring peaks, including the sprawling Nantahala, Plot Balsam, Bald, and Unaka mountains.

The rock core underlying this region is a billion years old. For humans, who measure time in the hours spent at work each week or the annual passages of birthdays, a billion years is beyond comprehension. The closest we may come to reckoning with this time scale is to look toward the undulating crest of the Smokies from the Foothills Parkway or the Gatlinburg Bypass, remembering the geological events that created these massive peaks required much more time than it will take for streams to carry them away chip by pebble until only flat land is left here. Unlike more rapid mountain building associated with western volcanic peaks,

upheaval and subsequent erosion of the Smokies occurred over so long a period that, if there had been humans here to witness the events, they would have detected little change within one lifetime.

The formation of these billion-year-old "basement" rocks began deep within the earth, where molten magma gradually solidified into granite. As the overlying crust slowly eroded, this core was uplifted as an extensive highland. Although most of this rock is now hidden beneath more recent deposits, examples of the core formation can be seen on the southern edge of Great Smoky Mountains National Park along Raven Fork and at the mouths of Deep and Cooper creeks.

About 800 million years ago, the region that would become the Great Smokies was flooded. Just the tops of the ancient highlands rose above this ocean. The only life forms that had colonized the land then were tiny bacteria and fungi, so unshaded rocks alternately baked in intense sunlight and chilled at night. Water froze, thawed, and froze again in minute crevices, ultimately splitting exposed cliff faces into smaller boulders and pebbles. Rain pelted the bare highlands, washing loose stones into rushing rivers. The stones knocked together, chipping off flakes that carried farther downstream. Eventually these mineral bits— quartz, feldspar, and clay from the original basement rock—were swept into the ocean.

For some 500 million years, particles flowed from the highlands to the sea. Animals including tiny clamlike ostracods now lived in submerged sands. Brachiopods and trilobites, half-dollar-sized creatures related to

Viewed from the Foothills Parkway, the undulating main crest of the Great Smokies reveals the rounded profile of an ancient mountain range.

horseshoe crabs, scavenged the ocean floor. As debris continued to flood down from the highlands, the calcareous shells of these and other sea creatures were trapped with sand, gravel, and mud particles in deposits four to six miles deep. The tremendous weight of the sediments caused buried layers to solidify into limestone, sandstone, and shale.

The formation of the Appalachians—mountains that eventually overtopped the ancient highlands in the Great Smokies region—is linked with these sedimentary deposits and with the geological theory of continental drift. In a simplified explanation, continents such as North America and Africa could be compared to rafts floating on a sea of molten rock, the Earth's mantle. These continental rafts, or plates as they are more properly called, may drift apart—with voids being filled by oceans—or may drift together to form supercontinents.

The North American and African continental plates collided about 300 million years ago, eliminating the ocean that formerly separated them. Layers of limestone, sandstone, and shale once deposited at the edge of the ancient Smokies highlands were squashed by the impact. Heat and pressure from this huge collision changed some sedimentary rocks, such as shales and sandstones, into metamorphic slates and quartzites. It also forced these rocks up and over the original basement core. Formerly ocean-bound rock layers were shoved northwest, with many being folded on top of themselves or coming to rest in a vertical plane. These crags, weathered over the eons, now delineate the crest of the Great Smoky Mountains.

After this continental collision heaved the Great Smokies upward, relentless freezing, thawing, and flowing water eroded the jagged peaks. In the process, cliffs and boulders have been reduced to gravelly rubble. Smaller rocks have disintegrated into the mantle of soil that blankets the hills and hollows.

"Anakeesta" is the name given to a prominent metamorphic rock formation in the park. Outcrops are dark and rusty-looking due to their high content of carbon and iron. In places sulfur mixed with the iron to produce shiny flakes of pyrite, or fool's gold. Slaty Anakeesta layers have come to rest at rakish angles along the crested pinnacles of Chimney Tops, the Sawteeth, and Charlies Bunion. These rocks break apart fairly easily and are prone to landslides, the scars of which

can be seen at higher elevations.

Another major component of the Great Smoky Mountains is the Thunderhead formation. This gritty sandstone is light gray and forms imposing bluffs such as those over which Ramsay Cascades and Laurel Falls flow. In the northeastern section of the park, Mount Cammerer, towering Mount Guyot, and Greenbrier Pinnacle are all capped by Thunderhead sandstone, as is Clingmans Dome. When the Thunderhead formation weathers, it breaks into angular boulders, some of which measure thirty to forty feet across.

It is typical for more recent rocks to rest on top of older layers. But in the Great Smoky Mountains, older rocks—such as the Anakeesta and Thunderhead formations—cover other newer layers, a result of the topsy-turvy buckling that occurred when the continental plates collided.

At Cades Cove, an even more unusual situation occurs. Younger rocks are visible through a "window," or huge break, in the continuity of the overlying older rocks. The smooth gray limestone on the floor of Cades Cove is only half as old as rocks in the mountains that encircle the valley.

Limestone is dissolved by flowing water and the weak acids that leach from plants. Farmers gravitated to Cades Cove before other areas of the Smokies were settled. Here they found deeper, more fertile soil, a by-product of weathering limestone.

Caves are unique to the Cades Cove area. Groundwater has etched underground passages in the limestone but not in more resistant sandstones, quartzites, and slates found elsewhere in the park. Unusual mosses, ferns, and orchids grow here, taking advantage of nutrients in the limestone-derived soils. Gregory Cave is the only place where a unique invertebrate, Gregory's cave amphipod, is found. Stupka's cave spider dwells in only a few of the caves in this region.

The southern Appalachians rise four to five thousand feet above the surrounding terrain. The normal weather pattern in this area sees moist, temperate winds swirling in from the Gulf of Mexico. When this warm, humid air flows up and across the cooler mountain slopes, precipitation occurs. At high summits, such as Clingmans Dome, the annual precipitation is about eighty-five inches. Excluding the rainforests of Washington's Olympic Peninsula, Smoky Mountain peaks are among the wettest areas in the continental United States. The valleys and lower slopes receive about fifty

The gritty sandstone of the Thunderhead Formation breaks into massive, angular boulders.

Above: *The freezing and thawing of water in rock crevices eventually splits cliffs into boulders and boulders into pebbles.* **Left:** *Slaty, mineral-rich rocks of the Anakeesta Formation are exposed at the summit of Charlies Bunion.*

Swiftly flowing water splashes across the bluffs at Ramsey Cascade.

The Great Smoky Mountains were not covered by glaciers. During the Ice Age, however, the climate here was cooler and wetter than it is at present.

inches of annual precipitation, usually delivered in the form of regular, gentle showers rather than gully-washing thunderstorms. The abundant moisture, fertile soil, and moderate climate of the Great Smoky Mountains combine to make this region a botanical showplace.

The biological diversity of the Smokies is tied to geological history. If we were able to return to the world as it appeared 65 million years ago, we would find North America and Eurasia attached where Greenland and Iceland now lie. The climate was warmer than at present. Broad-leaved trees, residents of temperate climates, flourished as far north as today's Arctic regions. In the Smokies, temperate vegetation grew on the higher slopes, while palms and other subtropical species covered the lowlands.

By five million years ago, the widening Atlantic Ocean separated Eurasia and North America. These continents were, however, joined by a narrow strip of land between Siberia and Alaska. The climate had

cooled considerably. Northern forests were cloaked with firs and larches rather than oaks and magnolia trees. Subtropical plants grew far south of the Great Smokies.

Cooling continued. During the Ice Age, which began about a million years ago, glaciers advanced south from Canada, Greenland, and Scandinavia. Huge ice sheets covered northern North America and Eurasia during these deep freezes, giving them an appearance similar to today's Antarctica. It is likely that cold air rushing off these glaciers lowered average temperatures in adjacent unglaciated areas as much as ten degrees Fahrenheit. The Great Smoky Mountains were never buried beneath ice, but the climate here chilled and received more rain and snow than now.

The glaciers advanced slowly enough that plant seeds and migrating animals could radiate outward ahead of them and survive. Appalachian mountaintops became an important avenue along which northern species traveled south.

During the coldest times, Smokies peaks over five

Overleaf: *Limestone rocks underlying Cades Cove are only half as old as the mountains that encircle this valley.*

thousand feet resembled today's alpine tundra communities with hardy lichens growing on rocks and a few other cold-tolerant plants. Northern animals such as snowshoe hares, spruce grouse, and snow buntings lived here. Although it is presently too warm for tundra to exist in the southern Appalachians, several of the highest peaks support relict lichens and mosses typical of polar regions. There would have been permanent snowfields at the heads of Smokies' hollows during maximum glacial advances. Spruce and fir trees at the upper limit of growth—probably three to five thousand feet—were stunted and gnarled by cold winds, ice, and snow.

The coves of the Great Smoky Mountains were less affected by advancing glaciation. Sheltered by bluffs and the thick forest canopy, local climates within the coves remained moderate. Rich soil and abundant rainfall allowed temperate species of trees and herbaceous plants to survive.

Four times the glaciers grew, with plants and animals inching south ahead of the advancing ice. Cold spells lasted as long as fifty thousand years. After each, the snow melted and life radiated north again. The most recent freeze cycle peaked about fifteen thousand years ago. As temperatures stabilized near their present levels during the past ten thousand years, temperate species spread higher into the mountains.

Continental drift and glacial advance-retreat cycles are responsible for some noteworthy plant and animal distribution patterns. As long as continents in the Northern Hemisphere were joined, they shared common flora and fauna. European wildflower guides reveal violets, orchids, buttercups, and hepaticas nearly identical to those of North America.

Interestingly, the same species of skunk cabbage grows in the eastern United States and in northeastern Asia, but not in Europe. Japan and eastern China are home to hemlock and tulip poplar trees, ginseng, trillium, partridgeberry, and Jack-in-the-pulpit flowers very similar to those half a world away in the Smokies. None of these plants is found in Europe either.

During the Ice Age, glaciers pushed flora and fauna south in the Old World. But in southern Europe, warmth-seeking plants and animals were blocked by the snowy east-west Alps and Pyrenees mountains. Many perished. In North America and eastern Asia, similar species were able to migrate along the north-south trending Appalachians, mountains of the Japanese archipelago, and highlands of central China to survive the advancing cold.

The Great Smokies are noted for several endemic species. Most are new on the evolutionary scale, probably isolated from relatives during glacial advances. They adapted to limiting soil, moisture, and temperature conditions in particular coves or highlands, evolving into different shapes, colors, and lifestyles than their ancestors. Rugel's ragwort, a plant with heart-shaped leaves and pale, thimble-sized blossoms, grows only in Smokies spruce-fir forests. Cain's reedgrass is also rare, found on a few rugged slopes including Mount LeConte and Charlies Bunion. Red-cheeked salamanders dwell exclusively in the Smokies.

The occurrence of northern flying squirrels, saw-whet owls, mountain paper birch trees, and twinflowers —all species at the southern extent of their ranges— also results from glaciation. These plants and animals reside on high peaks in habitats that are actually island outposts, similar to vegetation and climatic conditions farther north. Ancestors were forced south by glaciers. When the glaciers retreated, remnant populations lingered here in pockets of suitable habitat.

The geological history of the Smokies is marked by great changes: mountain-building, erosion, climatic fluctuations. We humans tend to perceive the passage of time and changes associated with its passage on a diminutive scale, such as the blossoming of spring flowers after a gentle rain or of saplings growing into a shady forest. On the geological scale, however, earthquakes, landslides, glaciers, and floods have irrevocably altered the face of these mountains. And it is these grand climatic and earth-moving changes—changes characterized as disasters on the human scale—that are ultimately responsible for the wealth of life that springs from the Great Smoky Mountains.

Above: *Red-cheeked salamanders dwell exclusively in the Great Smokies. (Photo © by Harry Ellis.)* **Right:** *Rugel's ragwort probably evolved from plants isolated during glacial advances. It is found only on high summits in the Great Smoky Mountains.*

Tulip trees bear teacup-sized flowers each spring.

AMONG THE GIANTS

"Connie, you really need to see those trees," said my friend Joe Abrell, coordinator of the resource management program at Great Smoky Mountains National Park. He was describing a virgin hardwood forest in the northeastern part of the park. "They're spectacular," he continued. "You just won't believe how magnificent they are until you see them."

Remembering Joe's suggestion, I gave the Albright Grove hike top priority on my next visit to the Smokies. In early June dawn filters into Cosby campground before six o'clock, but I didn't need an alarm clock. Staccato *zee-zee-zoo-zees* of black-throated green warblers filled the fog-drenched forest at first light. After breakfast, I left the car near Buckeye Lead and followed an old roadbed up a gentle grade.

The path threaded through a forest of mixed oaks and hemlocks with dense thickets of rosebay rhododendron in the understory. In the dim light below them grew glossy-leaved galax, indicating acidic soil, and carpets of partridgeberry.

About two miles from where I entered the woods, the old road narrowed. Here the character of the forest also changed. I was now surrounded by an impressive stand of tulip poplars. Most appeared to be of the same age—smooth gray trunks a foot to eighteen inches in diameter, rising arrow-straight at least fifty feet to the first branches. Within a few hundred yards, a large pile of rocks beside the trail confirmed my suspicions.

Some years earlier, very likely around the turn of the last century, the virgin forest on this gentle slope was harvested. Then the landowner and his family toiled day after day, picking up rocks, piling them on a wooden sled, and urging the mule to haul them to this dump at the edge of the field. Once cleared, the plot was plowed and planted in corn. By the time land for Great Smoky Mountains National Park was acquired in the 1930s, the farmer had sold out and moved away.

The cornfield was overrun by grasses and weeds the first year or so after he left. Gradually tangled blackberry vines and woody shrubs invaded this opening. On the sun-warmed soil beneath the shrubs, black locust, pitch and Virginia pine, and tulip poplar sprouted. The locusts and pines prospered during the first couple of decades while ample light beamed into the thicket. About forty years after the farmer left, however, the fast-growing tulip poplars overtopped the other trees. A close look beneath the shady canopy revealed ragged locusts and decaying, woodpecker-riddled snags of the outcompeted pines.

The form of their trunks told me this was a stand of tulip poplar. Had I instead peered into the canopy, I would have seen the squared outline of broad, four-lobed leaves. The trees are called "yellow poplar" by lumbermen, but the name is misleading. True poplars are members of the willow family. Tulip trees are magnolias, a fact obvious in spring when their teacup-sized flowers bloom. The misnomer may have originated because the large leaves of true poplars and tulip poplars, both attached to the branches by slender petioles, quiver conspicuously in the slightest breeze.

There was no breeze this morning. When I heard a twig snap to my left, I turned to meet the gaze of

Each spring, wildflowers of various shapes and colors highlight the understory of the cove hardwood forest. Among them are sessile yellow trillium (above left), Indian pipe (above right), rosebay (overleaf), and wild geranium (page 28).

a white-tailed deer some twenty yards away. Apparently I had been standing motionless so long the deer became curious. I remained quiet as it stepped gingerly around the rocks and inched closer, nostrils straining to catch my scent. Finally my human smell registered. The deer turned abruptly, flagged its tail, and bounded through the brush.

I continued up the trail toward Albright Grove. Throughout the morning, I listened to a symphony of spring bird songs. At this time of year, twenty species of warblers nest in the park. Each has a distinctive call, as do the orioles, tanagers, vireos, and liquid-voiced thrushes that share these woods.

The morning's most persistent chirps belonged to red-eyed vireos. These birds bounce from branch to high branch, looking for inchworms and other insect delicacies. Plumed in drab olive and buffy gray, they would be overlooked were it not for their songs. "I am here," they warble. "Here I am. Up here . . . see

me . . . here I am." Over and over the phrases are repeated, at the rate of about one per second. Songfests last thirty minutes to an hour, with brief rests, then more song. Red-eyed vireos utter more than twenty thousand "I am here" songlets each day of the breeding season. Their long-windedness has earned them the nickname "preacherbird."

Finally I reached a weathered marker where the path to Albright Grove diverged from the trail I had been following. In a few yards, as Joe Abrell had promised, I began to encounter some of the most magnificent trees in eastern North America.

Fertile soil, mild temperatures, and abundant moisture make the Great Smoky Mountains a tree-growing place. Here the mountains lie along a south-west to northeast vector, with each major peak eroded into various ramparts and coves. Instead of having one rather uniform surface exposed to cold north winds and the opposite south-facing exposure baked by the

Abandoned farmland is gradually invaded by woody shrubs, pines, and black locusts. Eventually these vegetative pioneers are replaced by fast-growing tulip trees.

summer sun, the terrain of the Great Smokies is a multifaceted complex of prominent ridges, sheltered slopes, and shady valleys. This topographic variety, which influences the intensity and duration of daily sunshine, combined with differences in rainfall and elevation, creates sets of conditions favorable to certain communities of plants and animals. The cove hardwood forest is one of these communities, and it is found only in the Great Smokies region.

Entering a mature cove hardwood forest is akin to walking into a cathedral. The pillared trunks of trees two to three centuries old support a vaulted roof of leaves high overhead. The largest trees are tulip poplar and hemlock, but the cove hardwood forest is known for its diversity. The richness of this forest is apparent when compared to other woodlands of the eastern United States. Elsewhere a quarter-acre sampling would normally contain about thirty types of trees. In an equal patch of cove hardwood forest, as many as seventy-five tree species may be present. Hallmarks include basswood, yellow buckeye, beech, white ash, Fraser and cucumber magnolia, sugar maple, and silverbell. Not only is the forest diverse, individual trees are much larger than those normally seen in eastern forests. Carolina silverbell, named for its dangling white blossoms, is a large shrub through most of its range. In the Smokies, it is not unusual to find towering silverbells with trunks two feet in diameter. Yellow buckeyes also grow better here than elsewhere. Mossy-barked giants reach diameters of three to four feet. More kinds of wildflowers are found beneath this forest canopy than in any of the other plant communities of the Great Smokies.

I hiked into the midst of Albright Grove and sat down on a fallen log. Around me in the lush understory were lace-doily leaves of maidenhair fern, toothwort, dutchman's breeches, and fringed phacelia. In bold contrast to this filigreed foliage were the broad, three-parted leaves of trillium, beds of stout trout lily leaves, and the unmistakable whorls of Indian cucumber. The majority of these wildflowers had bloomed in April and May, before the sun was blocked by the emerging canopy. A few vase-shaped Jack-in-the-pulpit blossoms remained. Several feet above eye level were hardy shrubs—plants such as spicebush and wild hydrangea—that survived in the dim light filtering through the canopy.

Most awe-inspiring were massive tulip poplars and hemlocks whose branches towered out of sight some 150 feet above me. These were trees too enormous to fit into one field of view. I sat facing a tulip poplar trunk that held enough lumber to build an entire mountaineer's cabin. Beneath the giants were sugar maple, white ash, and hemlock saplings, all remarkably tolerant of shade. They will thread upward into shafts of sunlight when older trees die, as the present behemoths prospered centuries ago.

The cove hardwood forest is a sanctuary. During glacial advances, magnolias, sweet gums, birches, sycamores, and several varieties of oaks—all known from fossils dating to the age of dinosaurs—took refuge in these milder coves. For millions of years the southern Appalachians have served as a genetic proving ground where these plants diversified to meet changing conditions. Each time the glaciers retreated, species sheltered here spread once more through eastern North America.

I remained for a time, looking around me at Albright Grove. Sometimes sight alone is not sufficient to digest the splendor of one's surroundings. I breathed deeply of the dank, woodsy aromas. Before I left, I reached my arms as far around the base of a big tulip poplar as I could. I stretched to barely a third of its circumference, but in so doing, my fingers embraced the wrinkled fissures of its bark.

I pressed my cheek close, as if hugging a venerable friend, and at that very moment a winter wren burst into song. Winter wrens are among the tiniest feathered residents of this forest community. They hop about on mossy logs and explore the margins of streams. Their song seems out of proportion to their size—a tinkling series of melodious trills that lasts far longer than a four-inch ball of brown fluff would seem to have breath. On and on it whistled, in an ebullient outpouring that filled the cavernous spaces beneath the trees, echoing the harmonies of the cove hardwood community.

Massive trees in the virgin forest at Albright Grove may have been saplings when Columbus sailed to the New World.

Among the two thousand varieties of fungi found in the Great Smokies is the lovely, but poisonous, fly agaric.

FOREST COMMUNITIES

Cove hardwoods are not the only forests in the Great Smokies. On the sunny ridges and south-facing slopes, pines and oaks dominate. Here summer's heat is intense, and the air is filled with the resinous, spicy odor of fallen pine needles. Hardy trees including northern red, black, and chestnut oaks, pignut hickory, red maple, and pitch pine are mainstays of the pine-oak forest. On dry ridgetops, trees do not attain the size of cove hardwoods, nor is their canopy as dense. Yet within this community is abundant life. Fragrant trailing arbutus is one of the first wildflowers to blossom each spring. Dainty yellow-fringed orchids flourish in midsummer's heat.

Amid the pine needles and decaying leaves grow myriad shapes and sizes of fungi. Coral mushrooms and tiny bird's nest fungi resemble their namesakes. Puffballs, possible to mistake for golf balls, grow nearby. Their spores develop inside, and the slightest bump puffs a cloud of ripe ones into the air.

Fungi have no chlorophyll and cannot make their own food. They survive because rootlike mycelia spread out in a wide underground network to absorb nutrients from the soil, wood, and fallen leaves. At certain times, often after rain, these nearly invisible mycelia produce the variously shaped reproductive bodies we call mushrooms. Mature mushrooms renew the life cycle by generating spores, from which new rootlets grow. Some two thousand varieties of fungi have been identified in the Smokies.

While walking in a pine-oak forest one spring morning, I heard a shrill *pee-tee,* the call of a broad-winged hawk. I followed the sound until I finally spotted the stocky bird on a branch of a red maple tree. Its keen eyes were alert to every movement. I suspected this hawk was a migrant, en route to a nesting destination farther north. Broad-winged hawks travel in loose flocks, following prominent landforms such as mountain ridges, coastlines, and river valleys on their peregrinations. It is not unusual to stand on Look Rock or some other high ridge in late March or mid-September and count several dozen broad-winged hawks passing by.

In distant views from Look Rock or Newfound Gap, the Great Smoky Mountains seem to be covered by a uniform green mantle flowing over the ridges and valleys. But when these grand vistas are reduced to intimate explorations, as in a hike from valley floor to mountaintop, the diverse character of each community is revealed.

For instance, you could be walking in a cove hardwood forest and gradually drop into a steep ravine where little sunlight penetrates. Here you might find a nearly pure stand of eastern hemlock. Hemlock seedlings germinate in shade more dense than most other trees tolerate. Graceful young hemlocks are easily recognized by their short, flat needles and the fact that new growth in the crown of the tree has a decided droop. Older hemlocks hold their lower branches long after those of other species die and fall off.

If trees have personalities, hemlocks could be characterized as patient. Saplings in the dark understory grow so slowly that a hand lens would be necessary to count their annual rings. Yet in places where overstory trees were harvested or died of natural causes, saplings respond to sunlight by growing ten times as rapidly as they did in the shade. Hemlocks are among the longest-lived trees in the Smokies. A few of the most ancient were young when Columbus discovered America.

Pure stands of hemlock are inhabited by exceptionally shade-tolerant understory species. The most common, especially along streams, is rosebay rhododendron. Rosebay blooms in June and July in clusters of pale pink flowers marked with green spots on the uppermost petal. Dog-hobble, a rambling shrub with leathery leaves, also grows here. Its name comes from early settlers who noticed their hunting dogs had difficulty tracking game through these jumbled plants. Nearby are rosettes of blue-green leaves netted with white veins. The overall pattern looks much like that of a coiled timber rattler, and for that resemblance, the downy rattlesnake plantain was named. This member of the orchid family produces a spike of tiny white flowers in midsummer.

Is it a curious coincidence that many members of the hemlock community are evergreen? Hemlock, rosebay, dog-hobble, shining clubmoss, and rattlesnake plantain all keep their leaves year-round. Perhaps where sunlight is at such a premium, the ability to make even small amounts of food during the winter gives these plants a competitive edge deciduous species do not possess.

Higher in the Great Smokies—usually above 3,500 feet and often on north-facing slopes where the air is cool and moist—grows the northern hardwood forest. In many respects, this woodland is similar to those of the northern United States and southern Canada. Among the dominant species here are American beech, yellow birch, striped and mountain maple, and yellow buckeye. Northern red oak, pin cherry, and a few red spruce trees are mingled throughout this forest.

The cool, damp climate encourages thick beds of moss to cover fallen trees, stumps, and boulders. The winged seeds of yellow birch often land on these spongy mosses and sprout. After two or three years, the seedlings' roots grow down and around the rock, stump, or log into the soil. In time, logs and stumps decay, leaving mature yellow birches seeming to stand on tiptoe. Even normally growing yellow birches are easy to identify. Their bronze bark peels into horizontal, papery

Hemlock trees grow in steep, shady ravines.

shreds. Broken twigs of yellow birch have the sweet aroma of wintergreen.

The northern hardwood forest is ruled by winter ice storms and high winds. Where trees fall, pin cherry colonizes. Also called "fire" cherry because it invades after fires, it produces clusters of bright red berries in August. The small cherries have an acidic taste but are relished by birds and bears. Hard pits pass through their digestive systems and are spread widely in droppings. The seeds sprout readily on bare soil, growing into a dense thicket that will persist two or three decades.

Beech and striped maple germinate beneath pin cherry and eventually overtop the twenty-foot shrub. Since its airborne seeds must land on ground warmed by sunlight in order to grow, striped maple is an indicator of past disturbances to a site. The bark of young trees is distinctively striped with vertical bands of green and white. A local name for the tree is "goosefoot" maple, referring to the shape of its leaves.

As in cove forests, the ground beneath northern hardwoods is strewn with spring wildflowers. Due to cooler temperatures at higher elevations, blooming dates for the same species of wildflowers can be as much as a month later in the high forest than on the slopes below. One of the first flowers to emerge here, usually in early April, is the spring beauty. With nutrients stored in a fat underground bulb, the spring beauty rapidly unfurls waxy leaves and delicate blossoms. The five-petaled flowers are decorated with fluorescent pink lines, or honeyguides, that radiate out from the center. Their function is to attract bees and other insect pollinators. Painted trillium, a dainty, three-petaled bloom of May and June, and wood sorrel, recognized by shamrock-shaped leaves, have similar patterns of magenta on white to guide pollinators to their centers.

Nowhere in the Smokies are microclimates—sheltered rocks at the base of a cliff, moist rotting logs, and shady stream banks—more important than in the harsh upper elevations. While a number of larger mammals, including black bears and red foxes, roam throughout the northern hardwood forests, it is generally smaller creatures, such as salamanders, that are particular about choosing a certain niche in which to live. Sleek Appalachian woodland salamanders are likely to be encountered beneath mossy, rotting logs in the park's higher forests. They are shiny blue-gray with a red cheek patch. Half a dozen of their close relatives, all uniformly dark in color, are found as isolated popula-

tions in nearby mountain ranges of North Carolina and Georgia. The red-cheeked form is limited to the Great Smokies.

Salamanders usually rest in crawlways beneath rocks or in rotting wood. They hide for good reason, as one of their most effective predators is a busy little mouse-sized mammal, the shrew. Pygmy, common, and smoky shrews reside within the park's high forests. Although they superficially resemble mice, shrews do not belong to the group of mammals called rodents but to those known as insect-eaters. They have pointed noses, beady eyes, and tiny ears. The pygmy shrew, only three inches long including tail, is the smallest North American mammal. It weighs only as much as a dime.

Shrews den in rotting stumps or logs and scurry about through the leaf litter. To maintain their exceptionally high metabolism, shrews eat twice their weight in beetles, earthworms, spiders, centipedes, and salamanders each day.

The influence of microclimates is also evident in the park's beech gaps. They are located in high saddles below mountain ridges, places subject to howling winter winds and unmerciful ice storms. Rather than the variety of northern hardwoods found nearby in more sheltered locales, the dominant tree here is American beech. Beeches, which in cove hardwood forests take on a grand, spreading profile, are here tattered and gnarled, with lichens clinging to their scraggly branches.

The flagged branches of spruces and firs, which grow above the beech gaps, tell an even harsher tale of gale-force winds, pelting thunderstorms, and weighty winter ice. The highest Great Smoky Mountains plant community is similar to boreal forests 1,500 miles north in Quebec, Ontario, and Newfoundland.

At the greatest extent of the last ice age, spruce-fir forests dipped as far south as Arkansas and Louisiana. When global temperatures warmed, spruce and fir retreated north to the Canadian shield and upward to mountaintops that average fifteen to twenty degrees Fahrenheit cooler than the valleys below.

Only seven "sky island" regions of the southern Appalachians host spruce-fir forests. The largest segment of this boreal forest—about seventy-five percent—is in the Great Smokies. Mount Rogers in Virginia, Roan Mountain in Tennessee, and in North Carolina the Plott Balsams, Grandfather Mountain, and the Black and the Balsam mountains are the other sites of spruce-fir forests.

From a distance this community is marked by dark, ragged spires of red spruce trees. Beneath the spruces, the Christmas-sweet odor of Fraser fir pervades the air. Spruce and fir are easy to distinguish by examining their needles. Remember *s* for spruce: *s*harp-tipped needles that roll between your forefinger and thumb to reveal four *s*quare *s*ides and crush with a *s*tinky *s*mell. For *f*ir, remember *f*: *f*lat needles that are *f*lexible and *f*ragrant. The small cones of red spruce hang down from the tips of the branches. Fraser fir cones point upright.

The harsher the climate, the less the diversity, so in this windy world only a few hardy trees coexist with the conifers. Among them are serviceberry (one of the first trees to bloom in the spring), mountain maple, yellow birch, pin cherry, and mountain ash, whose clusters of red fruits mature in September. Shrubby red-berried elder and witch-hobble grow in the understory. Witch-hobble's branches will root where they arch over and touch the spongy ground, creating a dense tangle that is easier to walk around than through. Branches were cut from these bushes by pioneers and hung near the mantle in the belief they would ward off evil spirits.

Sun glistens on the forest floor after a summer shower, highlighting raindrops on the lacy leaves of lady fern. Soggy logs are nurseries for a profusion of mosses. Individual moss plants are less than an inch tall and, if they did not grow in clumps, might go unnoticed. A close look reveals several types—some star-patterned, others feathery, still others with tiny fernlike leaves. Mosses colonize bare surfaces. Even though each plant makes a minuscule contribution, they build new soil by loosening bits of rock and adding decayed plant parts to it.

Many wildflowers of the spruce-fir forest are on an elfin scale. Bluets—four-petaled lavender flowers with bright yellow centers—are scarcely taller than the mosses. They grow in profusion around seeps and springs. Some settlers called them "innocence." Where sunlight lingers, taller flowers may be found. The showiest include the purple-fringed orchid, with massed blossoms on a stout stem, and scarlet beebalm.

When clouds envelop the mountains, your visual world closes to a small circle of dark-foliaged trees. As landmarks melt into the ephemeral mist, your sense of direction can become confused. Sounds are muffled. It is easy to believe you are the only living creature on

The wintergreen-scented bark of yellow birch peels in horizontal, papery shreds.

American beeches are grand, spreading trees in the sheltered cove forests. Higher in the mountains, where ravaged by wind and ice storms, they appear tattered and gnarled. Unlike most broad-leaved trees, beeches hold their golden leaves late into the winter.

Barred owls are efficient predators in the hardwood forests. They dine on mice, shrews, rabbits, and small birds.

A red maple leaf imparts a touch of autumn color.

this mountaintop. Then you hear a distant voice—or is it? Your ears strain to catch the sound. For a moment the silence is broken only by intermittent drips of condensed fog. Then the hoarse utterance comes again. Is someone calling for help?

"Gronk, gronk," the answer reverberates from just outside your circle of vision. The distant call was a raven, and now a mate is responding. While similar to the crows that inhabit lower elevations, the larger, heavier-billed ravens are more solitary and remain in the rugged highlands. On clear days, you will see them hang-gliding on updrafts over rocky promontories.

You may walk in silent wisps of fog for a while, and suddenly your ears will be assaulted by the loud, rattling call of the "mountain boomer." Aptly named, this chatterbox is usually heard before it is seen. When you finally spot it, it will likely be sitting on a branch above eye level, jerking its tail rapidly as it scolds. "Boomers" are more widely known as red squirrels, and, although found in lower forests, they seem at home among the conifers. They busily harvest the seeds from spruce and fir cones, as well as nuts, bird eggs, and fungi. They stake out favorite stumps and rocks, where they shuck seeds for hours. Their dining areas are littered with telltale husks, discarded cones, and nutshell castings.

While the red squirrel chatters, its smaller cousin the flying squirrel naps in an abandoned woodpecker hole. At dusk the roles reverse when the red squirrel retires and the wide-eyed flying squirrel ventures out to begin its nocturnal rounds. It bobs its head up and down to gauge the distance, then springs away from the tree and into the air with legs spread wide.

"Gliding squirrel" would be a more appropriate name, for the creature does not flap like a bird. Instead, it steers by stretching the parachutelike flaps of skin between its front and back legs and by ruddering with its bushy tail. A downward glide of twenty-five feet is about average. When ready to land, the little creature brakes by raising its tail, rearing up with its front paws, and impacting gently on all four feet. Habitually, flying squirrels race to the opposite side of the tree after landing, perhaps to foil any owls swooping down in pursuit. The squirrels often run up the trunk and spring into the air again, moving through the forest in a rapid climb-glide, climb-glide series.

Southern flying squirrels are quite common in the park, but because of nocturnal habits they are seldom seen. Slightly larger and darker, the northern flying

Above: *Red squirrels skillfully strip the husks from tulip poplar fruits and pine cones to reach the tasty seeds inside.* **Right:** *Tangles of mountain laurel and dense growths of rhododendron impede cross-country foot travel. Settlers referred to contorted stands of these shrubs as "laurel hells."* **Left:** *The ground beneath northern hardwoods and boreal forests may be strewn with wildflowers. Among the showiest is Turk's cap lily.*

squirrel resides in only a few areas at the edge of the spruce-fir forest.

If one were to overlay the ranges of the northern flying squirrel, the red squirrel, the snowshoe hare, and the northern red-backed vole on a map of North America, they would coincide—stretching across southern Canada and trending south in higher elevations of the Appalachian and Rocky mountains. Like the spruce and fir trees that surround them, these creatures are products of an environment more prevalent during glacial advances. As the climate warmed, they retreated upward and northward with the boreal forests.

Although no tundra exists above the spruce-fir forest, there are some fascinating treeless areas. Known as balds, they look barren from a distance. On close inspection, they are grass- and heath-dominated plant communities.

One summer morning, I set out along the Forney Ridge trail from Clingmans Dome, walking south to Andrews Bald, the highest grass bald in the park. Even though it was mid-June and already summer in the lowlands, this path at nearly six thousand feet was lined with bluets and other early spring bloomers. The leaves on the birches and serviceberry trees still had a tender green aura.

Although most of the trail traversed boreal forest, one section dipped into a heath bald or laurel "slick." Whoever coined the latter term was obviously looking from a distance! These areas contain head-high mountain laurels and nightmarish tangles of contorted rhododendron shrubs. I have never ventured more than twenty yards into a heath bald unless on a trail. To do so, you must claw over and around the branches, often dropping to your knees and crawling. Settlers referred to these areas as laurel "hells."

Beneath and around the rhododendron and laurel grow other members of the heath family, including blueberry and huckleberry shrubs, and sand myrtle, an evergreen inhabitant of Appalachian mountaintops and, disjunctly, New Jersey pine barrens. Why do so many types of heath grow here? The answer may have to do with their tenacious ability to colonize poor soil after a landslide or fire. It is also possible that Catawba rhododendron, which blooms with magnificent clusters of mauve flowers in June, has a toxin that leaches from fallen leaves to inhibit the growth of tree seedlings in the soil beneath these plants.

As I followed the trail through a tunnel of heaths, I heard the quickly whistled refrain, *please-please-pleased-to-meetcha*. The song belongs to the chestnut-sided warbler. A species that favors second-growth forests, the chestnut-sided is actually more numerous at present than it was before this nation was settled. The colors of a breeding male are breathtaking—jaunty yellow crown, crisp black eyeline and whisker markings, and rusty sides. When I came to an opening in the thicket, I made a few "pishing" sounds, imitating the noise warblers use to communicate boundaries of their home ranges with each other. In a moment the little bird appeared in front of me, flitting from side to side to show his gaudy plumage and singing to reinforce his territorial claim.

A few steps farther down the trail, I stopped to admire a dense cluster of mountain laurel blossoms. The wrinkled, conical buds are pink when tightly closed, opening into bowl-shaped white blooms with darker centers. On new flowers the slender stamens are attached in a radial pattern to pockets on the outer edges of the petals. I watched a bee land and probe for nectar. To my amazement, the pressure of the bee's touch loosened a stamen, which sprang forward, dusting the bee's side with a puff of pollen. The bee would be bombarded by more stamens as it gathered nectar and would rub against many sticky pistils, transferring pollen from one mountain laurel flower to the next.

About two miles from my starting point, I emerged from the darkness of the spruce-fir forest into an opening dotted with rhododendron and azalea shrubs. Before me spread Andrews Bald, about ten acres of grassland that afforded grand vistas of distant peaks. I walked across the uneven turf of matted grasses to the opposite side of the bald where some Catawba rhododendrons bloomed. Lavender blossoms hold a special attraction for butterflies, which are sensitive to wavelengths of ultraviolet light beyond the human visual spectrum. Several eastern tiger swallowtail butterflies loitered there on the sunlit flowers.

Before the afternoon grew late, I circled the bald, then retraced my steps through the waving sedges, grasses, and hawkweed. As I walked, I decided to visit another bald the following day.

It is a nine-mile round-trip to Gregory Bald via the Hannah Mountain trail, a steady gain of nearly 2,200 feet as the path winds up through pine-oak and cove hardwood forests into a beech gap and finally to the

The Christmas-sweet scent of Fraser fir and its upward-pointing cones identify this denizen of the boreal forest.

Above: *Salamanders live in moist crevices beneath rotting logs or along stream banks.* **Left:** *Bluets, also called "innocence," grow in profusion around seeps and springs.* **Right:** *Flame azalea, which blooms in May and June, was described by botanist William Bartram as "the most gay and brilliant flowering shrub yet known."*

mountaintop. The next morning I arose early and, while the morning air was still fresh, donned my pack at the trailhead.

The hike through the forest could not have been more lovely, as the flame azaleas were in full bloom. These shrubs, which range from five to fifteen feet high, were dappled with clusters of orange flowers. Discovered in the mid-1700s by father-and-son botanists John and William Bartram, the fire-shades of the "flaming azalea" were later remembered by William as "the most gay and brilliant flowering shrub yet known."

Azaleas were scattered throughout the forest, but when I reached Gregory Bald, they dominated the view, just as my friend Keith Langdon said they would. Keith is a natural resource specialist at Great Smoky Mountains National Park and an excellent field naturalist. Since coming to the Smokies in the mid-1980s, he has discovered nearly two dozen species new to the park, including several kinds of dragonflies, ferns, and wildflowers.

Every June, Keith treks to Gregory Bald to examine the azaleas unique to this mountaintop. According to Keith, many of the shrubs found here have hybridized among three or four azalea species. Instead of long orange petals with protruding stamens and pistils typical of the more widespread flame azalea, those of Gregory Bald have varying petal, stamen, and pistil lengths. Their hues range from blood red to golden-orange. Keith knows of one bush that has lemon yellow flowers. I found another with blossoms of rich pink. The plants here are so unusual that cuttings have been sent to the famous rhododendron collection in England's Kew Gardens for propagation and study.

Gregory differs in several ways from Andrews Bald. Andrews, at 5,860 feet, is slightly cooler, a bit wetter, and is dominated by sedges. Gregory, about nine hundred feet lower, is carpeted by mountain oatgrass, whose seeds resemble those of domestic oats. Mixed with this grass is a greater diversity of wildflowers than found on Andrews Bald. Low-growing blueberry bushes and the azalea shrubs are plentiful on Gregory Bald, while Andrews has more rhododendrons and mountain laurels.

No one can say for certain how the balds of the southern Appalachians came into existence. Most likely, both their formation and their maintenance relate to disturbances. Researchers theorize that openings in mountaintop forests may have been created by fires. Grassy plants were among the first to recolonize these areas.

A number of balds in the region are located on paths used by woodland bison and elk, grazers that would have kept the grasses flourishing. The bison and elk herds were decimated by early settlers, who replaced native grazers with domestic cattle and sheep. Every summer settlers took their livestock to the balds to fatten on the lush grasses. When the national park was established, grass balds were as smooth as baseball diamonds. Once set aside, the ungrazed balds began to grow up in a thicket of hardwoods.

Half a century later, without major fires or herbivores to keep them open, the balds are being encroached by hawthorns, oaks, and laurels. Using volunteers who cut back the invading shrubs and treat them with herbicides, the Park Service is maintaining Andrews and Gregory balds in as open a condition as possible. Other more remote balds, such as Parson, Siler, and Buckhorn, are dwindling in size. Perhaps reintroduction of bison or elk could revive these areas, but there are no plans to do so at present.

Before returning via the Hannah Mountain trail, I sat down on a rock in the midst of Gregory Bald. Around me in this sun-kissed meadow waved the ripening seed heads of oatgrass and the slender, brown-tipped stems of rushes. I was utterly alone, save for the brilliant azaleas and the indigo buntings that perched atop them to sing their buzzy songs. I could discern the dark forests below, with verdant fields of Cades Cove in the distance. Beyond them, a circle of hazy mountain peaks stretched well into Tennessee.

The scene was like looking at an impressionistic watercolor painting. From my vantage point, I could see the various plant communities of the Great Smoky Mountains. Each is unique, yet from this distance their singular qualities merged into a pattern of unity, just as the grand design of a painting emerges from the individual pastel brushstrokes. It is this diverse blend of components—cove and northern hardwoods, balds, boreal forests, and the myriad creatures that inhabit each community—that gives the Great Smokies such a rich natural heritage.

Distant mountainsides resemble impressionistic watercolor paintings, with each plant community displaying unique qualities of color and texture.

Four hundred to six hundred black bears live within Great Smoky Mountains National Park. Although most inhabit wilderness areas, bears are seen regularly at Cades Cove, along Roaring Fork Road, and near Greenbrier and Chimneys picnic areas. (Photo © by William S. Lea)

DISCOVERING WILDLIFE

The crags and hollows of the Great Smoky Mountains nurture a rich assortment of wildlife, from diminutive wood frogs and pygmy salamanders to four-hundred-pound black bears. On a typical walk you may encounter squirrels, chipmunks, and a variety of birds. Even though they are common, you are less likely to cross paths with foxes or bobcats. Many animal residents of the Smokies are wary of humans and hide quietly until danger is past.

Discovering wildlife here requires a mix of knowledge and patience. It is helpful to understand the physical requirements of each creature—to know, for instance, whether it lives near water or is active at night. If you approach stealthily, you may be able to watch an animal as it goes about its life relatively undisturbed by your presence.

My husband Pat and I shared such an experience one sunny November morning. We stopped at a woodlot along the Cades Cove road where on several occasions I had seen a young bear. We began hiking as quietly as the dry leaves beneath our feet would allow and had not gone far when Pat saw a silhouette moving through the shadows ahead. The bear turned to look at us, then raised his nose and sniffed. I have read that bears can discern the odor of a deer carcass as far as three miles away. Apparently familiar with people because its territory was so close to the road, this bear seemed to recognize that we were humans but did not react with concern.

We sauntered around the bear in a wide half-circle, putting the sun behind us. The bear looked up now and then but seemed most interested in pawing through the leaves. We crept closer. Through our camera lenses, we could now see that the bear was dining on acorns. In big, unhurried swipes, it raked the crunchy white oak leaves aside, allowing heavy acorns to roll to the ground. The bear's head was always moving, swinging from side to side as its sensitive nose sniffed for the nutty treasures. It seemed to smell and eat in one smooth motion, corralling the acorns with massive paws, picking them up between tongue and upper lip, crushing and swallowing, all the while allowing shells to fall out the sides of its mouth.

The bear was making lots of noise as it swished through the leaves but still relied on its keen sense of hearing to detect danger. Several times when noisy hikers and bicyclists (who were unaware of the bear's presence) passed by on the road, the bear stopped eating, lifted its head, and listened. To double-check these disturbances, the bear raised its nose and sniffed.

Studies of black bears have shown that adults lose from fifteen to thirty percent of their weight during their winter sleep. Thus it is imperative that they fatten up in the fall. Bears do not go into the same deep sleep as woodchucks or bats. They enter a cave or grass-lined earthen den, or climb as high as fifty feet into a hollow tree when autumn food supplies play out. Their body temperatures drop four to seven degrees Fahrenheit—in contrast to hibernating woodchucks, whose internal temperatures fall to just above freezing and whose hearts beat only five times per minute. Bears may awaken and even roam outside briefly on warm

Above: *"We watched the bear dining on acorns. It raked the crunchy leaves out of its way with unhurried swipes of its massive paws. Now and then, the bear raised its head and sniffed."* **Left:** *Black bears will travel many miles to find patches of ripe blackberries, blueberries, or fire cherries. On a diet of sugar-laden berries, bears gain as much as two pounds per day.*

winter days, but they do not eat, drink, or defecate during the entire hibernation period.

Female bears give birth in midwinter, while in their dens. Cubs are born blind and hairless. The groggy female rolls onto her side, warming the cubs by cradling them with her legs and chin. At the age of two weeks, smooth brown fur begins to cover the cubs. In another two weeks, their eyes open. By this time, mother may emerge from the den on short forays.

Bears are creatures of the forest, depending on trees for food, rest, and play. The number of offspring indicates the quality of a bear's habitat. Commonly, females raise one or two cubs. In the lush Smokies habitat, triplets are not unusual. In the Great Smokies, female bears reach sexual maturity at four to five years and have litters every other year thereafter. The youngsters suckle until midsummer and stay with mother the following winter. In the Smokies ninety-five percent of the cubs survive their first year, but once they leave mother's care, half of the yearlings die. Bears reaching the age of twelve are considered old.

Male bears, who roam across home ranges from thirty to forty miles in circumference, remain solitary except when courting. The female bear, limited to territory a third the size of the male's, plays the role of single parent, protector, and provider. She keeps the cubs nearby, directing them with grunts, or more seriously, with swats of her massive forepaws. If danger—especially in the form of a male bear who could kill the cubs—looms close, she will send them scrambling up a tree.

Should you encounter a bear with cubs, use caution that you do not come between mother and babies. Unlike with grizzlies, fatal attacks by black bears on humans are rare, but these animals are strong, quick, and unpredictable. If a bear seems disturbed by your presence, back away slowly to the safety of a tree or large rock. Staring directly into a bear's eyes may be interpreted as a challenge. Bears do not usually make noise when they play, so if you hear a growl or woof, it is a warning that you are too close.

Bears communicate among themselves by posturing and facial expressions. Raising or flattening the ears, for example, can indicate curiosity or anger. Males will turn sideways to give other males a good look at their size. Posturing avoids fights.

The bear we watched on that November morning had a thick coat that glistened blue-black in the sunlight. We guessed that it weighed about 175 pounds. Scientists in the Great Smokies have discovered bears here exist on a diet of four-fifths vegetation. They consume squawroot, or bear potato, when they emerge from hibernation, with a variety of insects, carrion, grubs, roots, and grasses. They do not regain any of winter's lost weight until summer fruits ripen. In the Smokies, bears will travel out of their home ranges to visit sunny ridges, balds, and burned areas where they feast on blackberries, blueberries, and fire cherries. On this sugar-rich diet, they gain as much as two pounds per day. Bears that appear scrawny in June can add a hundred pounds by late November or December.

The autumn bear was a hefty and lustrous contrast to a family of bears I encountered at the opposite end of Cades Cove the previous May. Late one afternoon, I noticed a scruffy female twenty feet up an ash tree near the Abrams Creek crossing. The emerging leaves were no larger than my thumb, but the big bear was pulling branches through her teeth, biting off the fresh greenery like corn on the cob. She was balanced on a surprisingly skinny limb for her size. Beneath her were sticks she had already gleaned, then dropped to form a rude platform that reinforced her perch. She would rise on her hind feet and reach as far as her front paws could stretch, grasping limbs two inches in diameter and snapping them off like matchsticks. When she did so, the tree swayed as if in a hurricane.

The female's twin cubs played quietly at the base of the tree. Occasionally one would scamper several feet up the trunk and hang on for a few seconds before backing down. The cubs were still nursing and looked well-fed. Their adorable little faces were embellished with rounded ears and dark, shoebutton eyes. Fifty yards away another skinny bear also sat in an ash tree, although this one hugged the trunk instead of venturing out on the pliable branches. It, too, broke off small limbs and consumed the new growth. From its size, I guessed this was a cub from a previous litter—now probably two years old. Mothers usually drive yearlings away before the next litter arrives, but sometimes they allow young females to share their territories. Both of these bears sat in their respective trees until well after dark, eating leaves as though they were famished.

Although many of the animals living in Great Smoky Mountains National Park dwell in the woodlands, Cades Cove—a lush valley—is one of the best places to see large species such as deer, bears, and turkeys. This

As afternoon shadows lengthen, white-tailed deer amble into meadows at Cades Cove and Cataloochee to graze.

was not always so, as pioneers cleared the level land to plant crops and raise stock. By the early 1900s, loss of habitat and overhunting reduced the numbers of deer, bear, and turkey so severely that they were seldom seen.

After the park was acquired in the 1930s, a few cabins and churches in Cades Cove were selected for preservation. When settlers moved away, abandoned fields grew up in dense, shrubby cover. To maintain the agrarian scene, pastures in the valley are kept open by local farmers who obtain permits from the park to graze cattle and horses or crop the hay. Deer, bears, and turkeys gradually multiplied in outlying forests and returned to the cove. Now they thrive along the interface of woodland and meadow.

Deer rely on leafy vegetation, which is more abundant in second growth and along edges than deep in the forest. But they seek the cover of denser woods in which to rest between meals. As afternoon shadows lengthen, deer rise from cool beds and amble into the meadows of Cades Cove to graze.

Deer may travel in herds of one to two dozen during the winter, but by fawning time they disperse. Does breed in their second autumn, bearing a single fawn the next May or June. Older does often have twins. The birthing process is quite rapid—a nearly bloodless event that takes only seconds. The youngster has no scent, and with nearly three hundred spots on its earth-colored pelt, it blends into the forest pattern of sunlight and shadows. These precocious little critters are able to stand and nurse within a few hours of birth, but they do not accompany mother until they are a bit older. The doe returns regularly, feeding the youngster milk that is nearly three times richer than that of a Jersey cow. The fawn grows rapidly. Within three months, it switches to a diet of leaves, grasses, lichens, mushrooms, twigs, and acorns.

During most of the year, bucks are recognizable by their antlers, which are outgrowths of bone. Old racks fall off in January and replacements, first resembling fuzzy knobs, appear in April. As they develop, they are sheathed in a tender covering of blood vessels known as velvet. The antlers grow several inches per month during the summer. In September, as male hormones begin to peak for the rut, the velvet dries up and peels away. Bucks speed this process by polishing their antlers against small trees. It is not unusual to see several sleek bucks prancing across the meadows of Cades Cove in the fall, vying for the attention of graceful does.

Wolves were once major predators of deer in the Great Smokies. In their absence, the size of the herd is now limited by food supplies and infrequent outbreaks of disease. Coyotes attack and kill deer occasionally, as do bears. On several evenings, participants in the hayrides that circle Cades Cove have seen bears dart out of the darkness to pounce on and kill deer.

Cataloochee, on the eastern side of the park, is another former settlement that has retained a number of open fields. It too, is an excellent place to observe deer. For a very few people, it has also been a place to see or find signs of another of the deer's predators, the cougar.

Mere mention of the cougar's other name, panther or "painter," was enough to strike fear in the hearts of self-reliant pioneers. These powerful tan cats can snap a deer's neck in seconds. They were, justly or unjustly, accused of killing children and livestock. Objects of intense hatred, cougars were thought to be exterminated from the southern Appalachians, but several reliable sightings have been made in the past few years. No one is certain if these are cougars of the same subspecies that originally inhabited the Smokies or animals somehow introduced from the West, where they are more abundant.

Turkeys are also wary animals, but they are seen regularly at Cades Cove, especially in the winter. Small flocks work the edges where field and forest meet. Waddling slowly, they scratch through the leaf litter, looking for acorns and beechnuts. They stretch their necks to pluck wild grapes and the buds of birch and ash. Venturing into the meadows, they glean grass seeds and insects in season. Their eyesight is keen, and their hearing excellent. If they sense danger, they run for cover, sprinting at speeds up to thirty miles per hour.

In late winter flocks scatter. Each tom struts to gather as many hens he can. His neck wattles, engorged with blood, turn brilliant red, purple, and blue. He fans his huge tail, drops his wings, and puffs out his chest, broadcasting a descending series of gobbles that can be heard up to a mile away. Although toms will fight with each other to protect their harems, the job of nesting and raising chicks is solely the female's.

The hen gathers leaves into a round nest, often in the lee of a log or stump. She visits the nest once a day for about twelve days in April, laying a buffy, speckled egg each time. When the last is deposited, she begins to incubate. In twenty-eight days the chicks hatch. They are soon ready to run behind their mother, pecking at small insects, seeds, and buds. Poults remain with their mother through the summer. Although eggs and young turkeys fall victim to snakes, skunks, foxes, and bobcats, survivors can live ten to twelve years.

Spring in Cades Cove is the time to watch for groundhogs emerging from hibernation. These overgrown squirrels weigh about ten pounds, and from blunt nose to bushy tail, they are covered with coarse brown fur. They live in tunnels that may go six feet deep and extend fifteen yards underground with one or two sleeping rooms. During the process of excavation, they move a third of a ton of soil, which is piled into a tall mound around an entrance. The groundhog uses this as a sentry post. Each tunnel has another hidden opening as an emergency exit.

Groundhogs have flat heads with eyes, ears, and nose far forward and close together. Thus they can peek over the edge of their holes to see if it is safe to go topside. They lope at only six to eight miles per hour so they usually burrow in a pasture, orchard, or near other reliable food sources. Woodchucks dine on grasses and succulent greens, but they have been known to shinny up fruit trees. Woodchucks can eat up to a pound of forage per day, a feat equal to a human eating a fifteen-pound dinner!

The Smokies take on a completely different aura on a moonlit night. The milky-white moon rises over distant peaks, haloing tangled branches and creating a lacy pattern of dusky shadows below. As the moon rises, it shimmers on rushing creeks and bathes the meadows in a glow of ghostly light.

This is the hour that many of the park's creatures begin to stir. The short-tailed, chubby pine mouse, for instance, may slip from its burrow amid the leaf litter of lower elevation forests. It eats seeds at the surface as well as tunneling to munch on roots, bulbs, and tubers. Higher on mountain balds the similar-looking southern lemming mouse may be tunneling through the turf. A seed-eater, this short-legged mouse cannot

Above: *Small flocks of turkeys glean acorns, beechnuts, and wild grapes at the edge of the forest. (Photo © by Maslowski Wildlife Productions.)* **Left:** *A sleek buck lopes across a meadow at sunrise. (Photo © by William S. Lea)*

reach the fruiting tops of most grasses. So it cuts the stems at the base and, when stalks tangle, keeps cutting at inch-long intervals until it finally pulls the seeds within reach. Piles of discarded stem pieces are left beside its runways.

As it scurries about after dark, the lemming mouse is fair game for owls. In the Smokies, the tiny saw-whet owl is limited to high evergreen forests. Screech owls, recognized by their small size and prominent ear tufts, are found throughout the park. Their quavering trill is a common component in the symphony of night sounds here. One of the most easily recognized soloists in this evening musical is the *who-cooks-for-you* hoot of the barred owl. They watch and listen for mice, shrews, rabbits, moths, and large insects that roam the deciduous forests.

Late evening is also the time striped skunks arouse from their dens. These heavy-footed, cat-sized mammals meander from one rotten log or stump to the next, digging for grubs and insects. If a mouse crosses their path, they will pounce on and eat it. In warmer months, they relish grasshoppers and the eggs of ground-nesting birds and reptiles.

Skunks are amiable creatures, perhaps because they are well-armed with a noxious sulfuric musk that can be squirted from glands at the base of the tail. Blasts of the macelike mist are accurate to about fifteen feet, temporarily blinding attackers. But skunks usually give ample warning before shooting—by turning around so the raised tail faces the intruder, stomping their feet, and sometimes even growling. Their only real enemies are great horned owls and foxes.

If humans possessed the nighttime visual acuity of an owl, we might watch a reclusive bobcat on the prowl. About twice the size of a house cat, bobcats trot slowly through the woods in a zigzag pattern. On a typical night, a bobcat might stop at a fallen log and sniff, placing its nose deliberately in several spots along the moss-covered windfall. Next it might tiptoe over to a stump, cocking its head and listening. It suddenly freezes in midstep, paw lifted, ears straining. In fluid slow-motion, it stretches low and begins to creep forward. Could we see its face, the pupils of the bobcat's eyes would be wide open, its pink nose scenting the air, and its whiskers bristling in anticipation.

Closer and closer the bobcat creeps without making a sound, until it is only five yards from an unsuspecting eastern cottontail. Then in a tawny blur with forepaws reaching wide, the bobcat makes two bounding leaps that result in a squeal and a fluff of gray fur. It ends the rabbit's life with a quick bite behind the neck.

Could we continue to watch, we might see this bobcat carrying her limp trophy back to the base of a rocky ledge. Two blue-eyed, spotted kittens bound playfully from a hollow log to greet her. Within a few weeks they will be old enough to follow mother on the hunt, but for now they are content to share what she brings back to the den.

Bobcats eat a variety of prey—squirrels, birds, mice, even lizards and insects—but their mainstay is the rabbit. In years when rabbits are abundant, more than two-thirds of the yearling bobcats survive. If rabbits are scarce, a high percentage of young bobcats will starve.

Pioneers used to brag that they could "lick their weight in bobcats," if they were good fighters. Bobcats usually slink away from confrontations, but if cornered, they can be vicious. Even their courtship is discordant. The female sits warily as the larger male circles her. They spat like domestic cats, only much louder, with vocalizations including snarls, hisses, growls, and high-pitched squalls. The courting repertoire can go on for an hour, a process the pioneers referred to as "caterwauling." It is not the kind of noise that would reassure you if you were walking alone in the woods on a dark night.

Opossums, which are slow-moving nocturnal animals, would seem perfect prey for bobcats. But opossums save themselves from becoming dinner by carrying out an elaborate ruse. The deception centers on the fact that bobcats will not eat tainted meat. Instead of trying to escape when threatened, opossums play dead. They fall to one side, lying absolutely still with eyes half-closed and mouth agape. They immediately defecate, which gives off a rotting odor repulsive to predators. No amount of prodding or poking can make them come to life. They remain "dead" from fifteen minutes to two hours after the attacker leaves.

Opossums differ from the other furry critters in the Smokies by being marsupials, or pouched mammals. Babies are expelled from the birth canal only thirteen days after the adults mate. This is comparable to a human fetus being born after eight weeks in the womb. Approximately twenty of these blind embryonic young are ejected at birth. The fortunate ones, roughly a third

Groundhogs burrow in pastures and near orchards. They consume as much as a pound of green forage each day. (Photo © by William S. Lea)

In fluid slow motion, a bobcat stalks its favorite prey, the eastern cottontail. (Photo © by William S. Lea)

Copperheads sometimes sun on rocky slopes or search for mice along wooded hillsides. (Photo © by Harry Ellis)

of the litter, pull themselves about two inches through the fur of the mother's belly into her pouch. There they attach to a nipple and suckle for about two months. When the babies reemerge from the pouch, they cling to the fur of the mother's back or to her prehensile tail, riding along as she forages. They grow to the size of chipmunks in the hundred days before they are weaned.

Interestingly, opossums have developed an immunity to the venom of pit vipers, which also hunt at night. There are two varieties of poisonous snakes in the Great Smokies—copperheads and timber rattlesnakes. The former are marked with rusty brown hourglass patterns on their bodies and have copper-colored heads. Timber rattlers range from yellowish with blotched black markings to almost entirely black. They are thick-bodied creatures with bony segments on the tail that buzz when vibrated.

Snakes are most likely to be seen around rock piles or logs. None of the varieties—poisonous or not— found in the park are aggressive toward humans. If you see a snake, skirt it. Although many people fear and kill snakes, they are actually an important link in the ecology of the area. Snakes eat a great number of rodents, and in turn serve as prey for larger animals.

One of the greatest treasures of the Great Smokies is that so many of the individual strands, so many of the interweavings in the region's web of life, remain. A few of the larger animals—wolves, elk, bison—are missing. But as a whole, the forests, meadows, and streams retain a full complement of plants and animals that interact with one another in much the same way they did before humans settled the area. Few other places in the eastern United States can claim this great a biodiversity.

Overleaf: *Opossums are the only marsupials in the Great Smokies. Babies take refuge in the mother's pouch for about two months after birth. (Photo © by Maslowski Wildlife Productions)*

RIBBONS OF LIFE

No plant or animal survives alone. Each is tied to others, in ribbons of life. A stream, as it flows from mountaintop to valley floor, forms a broad ribbon where many smaller strands gather and braid together. A tree, which grows, dies, and through the marvelous process of decomposition becomes a seedbed for a new tree, is another. In the Great Smokies, numerous ribbons connect plant to animal, animal to plant.

Imagine for a moment that you are sitting near one of the three hundred creeks that tumble through the park. This is sweet, pure water. The stream is swollen slightly by spring rains, but it maintains a transparency found only in pristine watersheds. The water splashes over mossy rocks and pours into quiet pools half-hidden by overhanging branches. Like distant laughter, the sound of the water whispers and surges. For many of the park's wild creatures, water is a magnet. It attracts frogs each spring to deposit their eggs. It draws deer for long, cool drinks on steamy summer afternoons. Dragonflies zip from bank to bank and dark beetles skate over the surface.

Near the headwaters of this creek, pools are small and cold. The water is slightly acidic. Beneath the glassy surface a streamlined brook trout faces the current. Olive-green speckled with red on the sides, flashy orange trim on the lower fins, the fish is no longer than a man's hand. If you sit motionless, it will cruise from rock to rock searching for crayfish, caddisfly nymphs, and aquatic salamanders. The trout flutters at the edge of the current, now and then snapping at mayflies, beetles, and spiders washed into the creek.

Brook trout inhabited many swift streams in the Smokies until the area was logged. Runoff sediments from the disturbed land then clouded the creeks. Loss of shady forest cover warmed the waters. Consequently, brook trout disappeared from three-quarters of their original habitat.

At one time brookies were so abundant that a local resident paid his dentist bill with two hundred fresh trout. Now they have been replaced by larger, more aggressive rainbow trout, a western species carried into the park in milk cans half a century ago to "improve" the fishing. Brown trout, a European species, were also released here.

Recently the National Park Service has been trying to bolster native trout populations. The first step is to identify creeks with waterfalls that will prevent rainbow and brown trout from swimming upstream. Then fisheries specialists walk the streambeds above these barriers, capturing and relocating the non-native fish. It is a tedious process, but it will give brook trout a reproductive advantage in the higher streams. Captured rainbow and brown trout are released downstream where sport fishing is allowed.

In addition to trout, other fishes in Smokies streams include shiners, brightly colored dace, sculpins, and river chubs. Beginning in 1987, several hundred smoky and yellowfin madtoms (tiny catfish) and spotfin chubs—all endangered species—have been released annually into their specialized habitat along Abrams Creek.

Fish feed upon a variety of insects, but one of the best-known—and most imitated by fly fishermen—is

As the Oconaluftee River flows through the Great Smokies, it draws myriad wild creatures to its clear, cool waters.

Above: *Native brook trout inhabit swift, tree-lined streams. (Photo © by Harry Ellis.)* **Left:** *Fishing spiders hide in vegetation at the water's edge. They capture insects, tadpoles, and tiny fish such as this dace. (Photo © by Harry Ellis.)* **Above right:** *The larvae of eastern tiger swallowtail butterflies feed on willow, birch, cherry, and poplar. Brightly striped adults warm themselves in the sun or sip nectar from wildflowers along stream corridors.* **Right:** *Damselflies rest with their wings folded back over their bodies, while their close relatives, dragonflies, sit with wings outstretched.*

the mayfly. Aquatic mayfly nymphs have long, flat bodies. They cling to rocks and underwater vegetation. Taking several years to mature, they finally crawl up a plant stem, split out of their skins, and emerge as winged adults. The inch-long adults are short-lived but highly visible as thousands gather in mating flights. Trout glean the nymphs underwater and rise to the surface to pluck floundering adults.

If you spend some time beside a still pool, you will likely notice six-legged water striders skating across the surface. Should you inch close enough, you will see fans of tiny, water-repellent hairs on their lower legs. The hairs give striders enough buoyancy to walk on the water. Dark, shiny diving beetles hang just below the surface, sucking air in through the tips of their abdomens. Whirligig beetles spin rapidly on the water. Their eyes are divided—half focusing into the air above the pool and the other portion scanning underwater.

Butterflies use the airspace above streams as avenues of travel. They may also be found in "drinking clubs" on wet streambanks. Swallowtails are especially prominent social drinkers. Male tiger swallowtails gather after emerging from their chrysalises. They remain together for hours, imbibing so much water that it drips from their abdomens. Some believe this is a cleansing ritual. Others feel that it keeps the males together until the later-hatching females emerge.

While butterflies visit streamside flowers for nectar, damselflies cruise the corridor above the water for living prey. Beginning life as aquatic nymphs, damselflies eventually climb plant stalks, shed their skins, and spread net-veined wings. In flight, they capture insects in a basket formed by their spiny legs. Damselflies are efficient predators, thanks to eyes with thousands of individual lenses, on heads that can swivel up, down, and almost completely around.

Another flying insect associated with stream corridors is the bald-faced hornet. Football-shaped hornet nests are often suspended from tree branches overhanging the water. The fertilized queen emerges from hibernation to begin the brood nest. She bites off bits of old wood and chews it with saliva until it is of papier-mâché consistency. The pulp is deposited in layered combs, covered by a papery shell. Inside, the queen lays one egg per cell. Each develops into a worker hornet.

Workers enlarge the nest and care for later broods. The workers dart in and out of a hole near the bottom of the nest on raids to capture caterpillars. They return and pull the prey apart, chewing it into pliable, bite-sized tidbits fed to new larvae. By summer's end, the nest may contain ten thousand hornets. The slightest disturbance—whether a raiding black bear or an unsuspecting hiker—provokes a stinging swirl of furious hornets.

Workers slacken their pace as fall approaches. Drones fertilize new queens, which will hibernate through the winter, but the rest of the colony dies off. Only then is it safe to pull down a branch to inspect a nest at close range.

Look carefully on nearby shrubs for the rough green snake. This skinny serpent is an excellent climber, but it also dips into the water now and then. Green snakes capture grasshoppers, crickets, spiders, and caterpillars by remaining motionless, like a vine draped across a branch, until unsuspecting prey ventures too close.

At night, common kingsnakes emerge from their lairs under logs to prowl the stream banks. They search for turtle and bird eggs and other snakes. Called "chain" snakes because of their cream-colored link pattern on a background of shiny black scales, kingsnakes are immune to the venom of copperheads and rattlers. They also prey on water snakes, subduing them by constriction before gulping them down headfirst.

Streamsides were likely places to encounter river otters before they disappeared from the Great Smokies half a century ago, victims of trapping and logging. By 1986 riparian habitat had recovered sufficiently to try an experimental release, so eleven otters captured in North and South Carolina were freed along Abrams Creek. In 1990 another twenty-five otters were delivered. Radio transmitters enable researchers to track their movements. Some have traveled as far as a hundred miles from the release site to set up territories. Pups have been observed, indicating the otters have paired and successfully settled into their new home. Studies show they are feeding primarily on crayfish but also consume stonerollers, hogsuckers, and white suckers.

Among the most distinctive birds associated with Great Smokies creeks are dapper blue-and-white kingfishers. These crested, flicker-sized creatures leave their streamside perches with an explosive, rattling call. They hover over the water, then dive headfirst to grab a minnow.

Green snakes, also called vine snakes, are excellent climbers. (Photo © by Maslowski Wildlife Productions)

Water is not the only magnet for wildlife. Although perhaps not as aesthetically pleasing as a trickling brook, a dying tree attracts a spellbinding array of creatures large and small. In the Great Smokies, individual trees may grow and prosper for two to three hundred years before they succumb to a lightning strike, disease, or old age. About one percent of the trees in virgin forests here die annually.

Trees age as humans do. Like a child, a sapling grows rapidly. A mature tree may live healthily for decades, but eventually it loses vigor. Instead of showing gray hair and wrinkles, an aged tree develops dead branches as a result of a gradual decrease in the transport of nutrients from the roots up through the capillaries beneath the bark. Older trees are also less able to repel insects and diseases.

A healthy tree—covered by tough, watertight bark—stands as a fortress against fungal spores and most insects. But if a windstorm tears a branch, a fire scars the trunk, or a squirrel gnaws into the bole, agents of decay may gain a foothold. Trees do produce chemicals to inhibit decay and grow new bark and cambium to cover wounds. Replacement calluses take a few weeks to several years to form, depending upon the size and jaggedness of the wound.

Carpenter worms and flat-headed borers are among the insects that attack live trees. These hungry grubs enter through the lower trunk or roots. Carpenter worms, which eventually hatch into adult moths, eat their way deep into the wood. Two-lined chestnut borer larvae girdle trees by making meandering feeding tunnels beneath the bark. Yellow-bellied sapsuckers also penetrate live trees. These woodpeckers drill evenly spaced rows of holes that spiral around trunks and large branches. They return periodically to lap up sap that drips from the holes as well as to eat gnats and ants attracted to the sweet liquid.

Once patches of bark have been loosened, the door is open to all types of invaders. Carpenter ants set up residence in the damp wood, rasping out honeycombed

Individual trees may prosper for two or three hundred years before they die and gradually decay. In the process, they provide food and refuge for countless other creatures.

Northern flickers feed on ants and beetles gleaned by drilling into insect-infested trees.

Conks, the shelflike fruiting bodies of wood-rotting fungi, often emerge from the bark in summer or fall.

chambers for fertile queens. Hard-shelled bark beetles burrow beneath the loose bark. They gnaw patterned galleries in which females lay eggs.

Bacteria and fungal spores hitch rides on these insects. Once inside moist galleries, they multiply rapidly. Enzymes produced by some of the microscopic invaders soften the wood and allow it to rot more rapidly. Some fungi and bacteria have mutually beneficial roles with insects. Tunneling insects also carry tree diseases. The elm bark beetle, for instance, is the vector of Dutch elm disease, the killer of millions of American elm trees.

The sound of insects chewing beneath the bark attracts woodpeckers. (If you doubt this, sit quietly among some dying trees!) Woodpeckers also tap briskly on tree trunks and branches, then listen. The tapping vibrations awaken resting larvae, which begin to move with faint ticking noises.

When a woodpecker suspects an insect is beneath the bark, it anchors itself with hooked claws, braces with strong barbed tail, and begins to hammer the bark with its chisel-shaped beak. Woodpecker skulls are similar to football helmets; the brain is surrounded by a narrow space, cushioned within a spongy bone casing. Strong neck muscles—like the thick necks of football linemen—absorb much of the shock of drilling as the birds' bills strike wood at about fifteen miles per hour.

Even though woodpeckers pound holes in trees, their role is often that of a healer. Woodpeckers are so efficient at seeking out insect invaders that ailing trees may recover. Woodpeckers usually begin feeding at the base of a trunk, spiraling around and into the upper branches, then swooping down to the base of the next tree. Flickers are particularly fond of carpenter ants, which they collect by inserting long, sticky tongues into ant galleries. Downy and hairy woodpeckers dine on bark beetles and larvae. The largest of the Great Smokies woodpeckers, the crow-sized pileated, feasts on ants and grubs.

Not only do woodpeckers tap into trees for their meals, they also excavate holes large enough to nest in. Woodpeckers use both live and dead trees for nests. Construction typically takes a week or two, and usually a pair of woodpeckers will make a new hole for each nest. Once abandoned, their holes are appropriated—depending upon their size—by gray or flying squirrels, screech owls, nuthatches, titmice, chickadees, or bluebirds.

An opening the size of a woodpecker den is likely to act as a window for heartrot and other types of fungal decay. Minute spores of rot-causing fungi are wind-blown from woody mushrooms, called conks, growing on nearby trees. After a heartrot spore enters a tree, it germinates. First a single filament grows from the spore. Filaments multiply, reaching deeper into the heartwood as they absorb nutrients. Wood fibers are weakened, turning soft or brittle, brown or white. Sometimes a rotting tree will have a sunken, cankerous surface around the original wound. Often in summer or fall new conks emerge as shelflike growths on the bark of the dying tree.

Hollow trees may stand for years, serving as homes for birds, squirrels, raccoons, opossums, or black bears. Finally the snag weakens and falls. Once on the moist ground, the process of decay accelerates. A snag that drops across the face of a slope rots before one that points up or down hill because it traps fallen leaves and soil. Squirrels, mice, rabbits, snakes, and myriad other animals rest briefly in the shelter of the log. They may defecate or groom themselves, spreading seeds and spores they have ingested or brushed against.

By mites and springtails so tiny they can barely be seen and by sowbugs, ants, earwigs, and earthworms, the fallen log is invaded. More types of bacteria, fungi, yeasts, molds, lichens, and mosses colonize the log. Snails roam here, especially at night or after a rainshower, moving along on a muscular foot, leaving a shiny trail of mucous. They rake off bits of plant material with their sharp tongues. Millipedes, too, graze on the decaying vegetation.

Salamanders take refuge in rotting wood. Among their preferred foods are wireworms, such as the larvae of the eyed elator, a wood-dwelling beetle with false eyes on its carapace. Female box turtles seek decaying logs when it is time to lay their round white eggs. Digging is easy here, and the eggs stay moist until they hatch—unless they are discovered by a skunk or bear, both frequent diners at windfalls.

When a magnificent old tree crashes to the ground, it opens a window in the forest canopy. Around the stump, soil has been enriched by composted leaves accumulated during the tree's life. In this humus sprout wildflower seeds, hickory nuts, and acorns forgotten by squirrels. Then fungi in the log have one more role to play. Their hyphae, the threads of their rootlike mycelia, surround the roots of these new seedlings,

Overleaf: *Eastern box turtles roam during moderate weather, but return to burrows under rotting stumps and logs to pass periods of extreme heat or cold.*

Above: *Snails roam about on fallen logs and nearby mushrooms.* **Left:** *Hollow cavities in trees may serve as homes for raccoons, squirrels, or bears. (Photo © by William S. Lea)*

When a mature tree crashes to the ground, it opens a window in the forest canopy. The decaying log will nurture a variety of plants. It may eventually give rise to a seedling that will replace the fallen tree.

Acorns that escape being eaten by insects, turkeys, deer, bears, or squirrels may sprout and grow into new oak trees.

helping them absorb moisture and nutrients from the soil. In a mutually beneficial relationship, seedlings relinquish sugars stored in their roots to feed these fungi.

Through its death, one tree touches the lives of countless other plants and animals. A fallen tree is an excellent reminder that there is no waste in the forest, only a wondrous process of recycling. It is hard to pinpoint when the tree's former life ends and its new life begins, since what some might call rotten wood is really a future generation of the forest.

In order to discover the countless ribbons of life that link plants and animals of the Great Smoky Mountains, all you need to do is choose a strand. A stream, a tree, even something as simple as an acorn will do. Then spend a little time observing.

Ten species of oaks grow in Smoky Mountain forests. About the time spring leaves are the size of a squirrel's ear, mature oaks bloom. Their tiny flowers are easily overlooked, but by early summer oval fruits are obvious. Acorns of the white oak group, oaks with rounded leaf lobes, are sweet-tasting and ripen in one season.

Red oaks, recognized by sharply pointed leaf lobes, have bitter acorns that require two years to develop.

Only a few of the acorns produced by mature oaks generate new trees. While still green, about a third are attacked by acorn weevils. These insects are half an inch long, but they have large, downward-pointing snouts used to drill into the hull and rake out the nut meat. Female weevils deposit an egg in the cavity after their meal is finished.

Each egg hatches into a small white worm, which eats more of the acorn meat. When the nut finally falls to the ground, the jolt triggers the larvae to gnaw from its casing and bury itself in the soil to overwinter. Pick up a few fallen acorns the next time you walk in the forest. Many of them will have holes in the sides where acorn weevil larvae have exited.

Squirrels scamper about in the branches of oak trees, harvesting acorns as they ripen. Gray squirrels bury individual nuts for use later in the winter. About ninety-five percent of these acorns are found and eaten, but not necessarily by the squirrel that hid them. Gray squirrels have an excellent sense of smell, detecting

Black bears seek acorn-laden trees each autumn. They gorge themselves on the tasty nuts, adding the extra fat needed to see them through a hard winter.

acorns and nuts even when buried below soil and snow. Red squirrels cache their acorns in wide, gently sloping midden piles. Should a roaming black bear discover the ground-level cache, it will feast while the red squirrel chatters bitterly from a nearby branch. Once the bear has left, the squirrel will take any remaining acorns and hide them in a new midden.

One of the best places to watch wildlife in autumn is under a white or chestnut oak tree. I have seen hungry bears rear up on their hind feet, reaching as high as they can to pull down acorn-laden branches. Deer munch the nuts with as much relish as (and more noise than) a hungry hiker snacking on a granola bar. Blue jays land beneath the trees, gulping down half a dozen or more acorns at a time to fill their crops. For good measure, they usually grab one more in their beaks and fly away to hide it in a tree crevice for a later snack. Wild turkeys and grouse shuffle through the leaves, searching for the nutty delicacies. At night, white-footed mice also gather acorns, eating some and burying the rest.

Insect-infested and partially eaten acorns may appear to lie discarded on the forest floor. But look at them closely. A host of secondary feeders move in to use the remainder of the food energy held in these large nuts. You may find predatory wasps hunting weevil and acorn moth larvae. You may see ants, tiny springtails, and maggots. Centipedes poke their heads into broken shells, searching for tinier animals hiding inside. Slugs and snails graze on decaying nut meats and on the fungi that decompose them.

A few acorns survive uneaten and sprout the following spring. Even they have "house guests." The acorn provides a bit of food and refuge to tiny insects and bacteria that enter beneath the cap or through the split in the shell. Meanwhile, the seed grows unharmed by their presence into a sapling.

As the years pass, ribbons of life intertwine with this young tree while it matures, dies, and decays. But the "death" of an aged tree is a somewhat superficial loss, since it is actually a life-giving event for countless other plants and animals. In the wider view, there is no real death here, only changes from one form of life to the next.

When Europeans encountered the Cherokees, the Indians lived in streamside villages and grew crops of corn, beans, and squash.

VOICES IN THE WOODS

For uncounted centuries, plants and animals of the Great Smoky Mountains lived with one another in a realm unseen by human eyes. No one can say when the first people wandered into these valleys, but nomadic bands of hunters could have roamed here as long as ten thousand years ago. The explorers knew how to make crude shelters and clothing, kindle fires, and chip flint into sharp points with which to kill game. Relatively little else is known about these mountain dwellers except that their numbers were few and their influence on the land was minimal.

By a thousand years ago, human inhabitants of the southeastern forests had domesticated dogs, learned to make pottery, and were growing plants such as corn and sunflowers. Some of these people became known as Cherokees.

When European explorers encountered the Cherokees, the Native Americans dwelt in log huts in small, streamside villages. The men hiked into the mountains to hunt game and seek spiritual guidance. Women and children tended patches of melons, squash, corn, beans, and tobacco. Fish, nuts, and berries—all obtained nearby—supplemented their diets. Pelts of deer, beaver, and bear were used to make clothing and for trade.

The Cherokees were a fairly peaceful tribe with rich cultural traditions. They believed in a single god and developed a democratic governmental organization. Women participated in tribal affairs as equals with men. Sequoia, a brilliant Cherokee thinker, invented an alphabet. Within two years after his symbols were presented to the tribal council, most Cherokees learned to read and write.

Although the east coast of North America was populated by Europeans in the 1700s, the rugged mountains remained Indian territory. Following the Revolutionary War, however, an increasing number of colonists hungered for new land. Restless settlers explored west from Charleston, South Carolina, and down through the Shenandoah Valley from New York and Pennsylvania. They were joined by emigrants from Germany, Scotland, Ireland, and England seeking to make a new life.

Huge tracts of virgin woodland covered this interior wilderness. Panthers and wolves lurked in the shadows; flocks of passenger pigeons blackened the skies. Faced with rugged terrain, the settlers worked their way along the rivers and up the valleys, where they found scattered Cherokee villages. Some distrust and skirmishing occurred on both sides, but the land here was bountiful enough for the Cherokees to share with the newcomers. As a matter of fact, if the settlers had not listened to the advice of the Indians, they might not have survived. Cherokees showed them herbs they could eat and use as medicine. For a while, the two cultures coexisted in relative friendship.

Pale-skinned settlers reached Cades Cove and Oconaluftee in the 1790s. By 1802 the first white child was born in White Oak Flats, a community that gave rise to Gatlinburg. John Oliver filed a land claim for Cades Cove in 1818. Within the next decade, many hollows in the Smokies had new cabins being built.

As more settlers arrived, the Cherokees were asked

Although the Cherokees helped the first white settlers who came to the Great Smokies, the Indians were later evicted from their traditional homeland.

European settlers cleared land in fertile valleys, such as Cades Cove, and led self-sufficient lives. (Photo © by Pat Toops)

John Oliver, a veteran of the War of 1812, brought his family to Cades Cove. This hand-hewn cabin was built in the mid-1800s to replace Oliver's earlier home.

to sign treaty after treaty. Each time they lost land and rights. Later settlers disregarded the aid Cherokees provided to the first Europeans. The Indians were stripped of all holdings by 1828. A few years later gold-seeking whites marshaled the Cherokees out of their homes to be herded on what became for many a death march to Oklahoma. A few Cherokees fled to Shaconage, their mountain refuge in the heart of the Smokies, where they hid. Several years later they and some of the Oklahoma Indians moved to the Qualla Reservation, set aside for them at Cherokee, North Carolina. Their descendants still live on this eastern slope of the Great Smokies, blending traditional dress, language, and life-styles with tourist-oriented businesses that help to support the tribe.

The early 1800s marked the dawn of a new era in the Great Smoky Mountains, an era when it was not unusual to hear the sounds of human voices in the woods. What did the emigrants think about as they trudged upward beside gurgling streams? For buckskin-clad men with flintlocks in hand, was there a sense of adventure as they followed dwindling trails deeper into the unknown? Did their new brides sometimes pine for a mother or dear sister and the comforts of the homes they left behind? Pioneer women must have wondered if the barrel of flour would hold out until the crops were harvested. Did they take stock of the simple provisions in their wagons—coffee, salt, an iron cooking kettle, precious garden seeds, a hoe, an ax, the Bible—and question whether their faith and self-reliance would see them through the rough times ahead?

Ingenuity and pride in a hard day's work were hallmarks of these settlers. They were independent, clever people who took materials from the forest and transformed them into food, shelter, and clothing. Of necessity, they lived close to nature. There were no doctor's offices or hardware stores down the block. If the settlers could not make do, they did without.

79

The initial priorities were food, water, and shelter. Building a home began with the laying of a stone foundation and hearth, topped by a rock chimney chinked with clay. The homesite was usually located near a spring or stream. Tulip poplars would be felled and split for puncheon flooring—boards three feet wide and four inches thick. Chestnut trees provided massive logs, split and side-matched, hewn square with a broadax, the ends carefully dovetailed. Neither of these trees were desirable as firewood—chestnut throws sparks and tulip doesn't heat well—but together they made a cabin that would withstand the rigors of weather and insects for a hundred years. Roofing "boards" would be rived from white oak. Door hinges and latches might be hand-carved from wood or fashioned from leather. Pioneer homes were elegant in their functional simplicity.

Corn was the major crop, relatively easy to grow in small forest clearings. The first harvest was fresh roasting ears in midsummer. The remainder matured into dry kernels that didn't spoil easily. Corn could be ground into meal using homemade, water-powered tub mills. "Mill Creek" is a common name in the Smokies because at one time there was a tub mill for each small cluster of homes. Corn bread, corn dodger, mush, and corn pone were staples at pioneer tables. Corn fodder was fed to livestock. The grain was used to fatten hogs before butchering and was sometimes made into mash. Mash was distilled into whiskey, a compact item that could be carried out of the hollows once or twice a year to trade for coffee, salt, and the few other items settlers could not make on their own.

A typical homestead included a snug cabin and a log barn with stalls where a dairy cow, a couple of pigs, and a span of oxen, mules, or work horses might be housed. Under the barn's peaked roof was a loft to store hay. Parked in the wide center aisle between the stalls, or perhaps beneath a lean-to on the side, were a wagon and animal-drawn farm equipment such as a plow and a hauling sled.

Several paces away stood the woodshed, a three-sided affair with rounds of hickory firewood piled near a chopping block out front. Inside rose stacks of neatly split pine kindling and dry wood for the cookstove. On the walls, suspended by pegs, hung an array of homemade wooden mallets and rakes. Beside them were hoes, scythes, and saws with precious iron blades. Their handles were fashioned from seasoned hickory or white ash, worn to a smooth, sweat-stained finish

by countless hours of use. Wooden nest boxes for the hens lined the back wall.

The smokehouse was a few steps from the cabin. It was stoutly built to keep out bears and winter's cold. In one corner rested a hollow tulip poplar log filled with salt. Salt was generously rubbed into freshly butchered hams, shoulders, and "middlin's" (bacon) which were then laid on shelves to cure.

Hog butchering was hard work, a good excuse for neighbors to gather and share tasks. Pioneer families prided themselves on using "everything but the squeal" when they butchered. Fat was saved for lye soap, cleaned intestines were filled with sausage, meat from the head was made into souse, or headcheese. Even the hog's bladder was cleaned, inflated, and used by the children as a ball.

Butchering began with the onset of cool weather in November, taking advantage of natural refrigeration. If meat was left when the warmer days of spring arrived, it was washed, coated in brown sugar and black or red pepper, then hung with white oak cordage from the rafters of the smokehouse. A low fire of hickory chips was kept smoldering there for a few days until the meat cured.

Some smokehouses had a trap door that led to an earthen pit where settlers stored turnips, potatoes, and cabbages. Other homesteads had a separate root cellar for the storage of garden vegetables. Wooden barrels of dried apples, peaches, and blackberries, crocks of kraut, and jars of pickled beans lined the walls. Strings of beans, peppers, slices of pumpkin, and braided skeins of onions dangled from the rafters. Pioneer families toiled from early spring into fall tending and preserving a harvest that would see them through winter. As the days grew cooler and shorter, one measure of a family's wealth was how well-stocked its root cellar was.

By spring, however, everyone tired of salt pork and dried beans. When the first green shoots of wild mustards, cresses, and brook lettuce sprouted, eager hands immediately plucked them for the table. Families hiked up into the mountains to dig ramps each spring. The bulbous roots with garlic-scented leaves were eaten raw and cooked.

Spring was also the time to give the cabin a thorough cleaning. Younger children helped carry the table and ladder-back, hickory-bottom chairs from the kitchen and sitting room, while an older one kindled a fire under the big, black wash kettle in the back yard. Mat-

Ingenuity and hard work marked the settler's lives. They transformed resources from the forest into food, shelter, and clothing.

Corn was a staple crop. It could be ground in simple tub mills or taken to a larger community mill.

tresses (made from feedsacks) were handed down from the loft, dragged outside, and emptied of their year-old straw stuffing. Fresh straw from the newly thrashed winter wheat was used to refill them after the covers were washed. Feather beds, tickings filled with goose or duck down, flapped in the sun. When the cabin was emptied, the bare wooden floors were scrubbed spotless with lye soap and a cornshuck mop. By nightfall everything was back in order, and the tired family fell asleep to the fresh scent of the outdoors in their quilts and bedding.

Although children were needed at home to help with chores, parents also realized the necessity of formal schooling. Many mountain communities had subscription schools during the winter months. The teacher was paid and boarded by parents. Some churches doubled as classrooms. Larger communities, such as Cataloochee and Cades Cove, had separate schools. Reading, arithmetic, spelling, and grammar were taught to the younger children, while older ones also studied geography and history. Since a teacher might be in charge of thirty to forty children of various ages, older students helped younger ones with their lessons.

Travel was limited in those days because the roads were so poor. The first trails followed rocky river beds so as not to consume cleared, level farming sites. Most people walked if they had to go somewhere, although horses or mules were used to pull wagons carrying trade goods. On rare visits to see relatives in other communities, paw might put straight chairs in the wagon bed to seat grandparents or in-laws, while the children alternately bounced with them or ran ahead. Top speed was ten to twelve miles per day.

As the years passed, men of each community gathered periodically for "road workin's." They moved rocks, filled holes, and leveled trails as best they could with hand and horse-drawn tools. When they could afford it, they used blasting powder to dispatch large boulders. Poorer road crews built bonfires against the big rocks, then poured cold water over them to crack off manageable chunks.

In such isolated conditions, it is no wonder that few people sent to the cities of Knoxville or Maryville for a doctor when a relative became ill. A common remedy for coughs was an elixir of cherry bark sweetened with honey. Juice of touch-me-not was rubbed on skin exposed to poison ivy. For ague (flu), the patient's feet were soaked in hot water and willow tea administered.

Central to the homestead was a barn where livestock was housed and hay was stored.

Living in relative isolation, mountaineers developed home remedies. Among their medicinal plants were golden seal (above), jewelweed (right), and tansy (page 87).

Dropsy (weak heart) was treated with purple foxglove tea; stomach ache with tea made from golden seal roots. For colds, the patient might be given a drink of kraut brine. Yellow jaundice was treated with a mixture of ground sow bugs and molasses.

The effectiveness of some remedies is questionable, but many actually worked. Willow bark, for instance, is the source of salicin, nature's equivalent to aspirin and a perfectly acceptable treatment for the flu. Purple foxglove contains digitalis, still used in the treatment of heart problems. A cold sufferer given salty kraut brine gets thirsty; drinking plenty of fluids is a cold treatment suggested by doctors today. Counteracting poison ivy with jewelweed works because acids in one plant's juices are neutralized by bases in the other. Perhaps by trial and error, the mountain people were able to heal themselves using a variety of plants from the fields and forests beyond their doorsteps.

To be certain, settlers died in spite of, or perhaps because of, home remedies. Sadness surrounding the death of a neighbor was shared by the whole community, as were the tasks associated with the funeral.

The death announcement was broadcast by ringing the bell at the deceased's church. Initial pulls on the bell rope got everyone's attention. A short silence was followed by a somber sequence of tolls equal to the dead person's age. Since most deaths were preceded by lingering illness, neighbors and relatives knew at once who had passed away. Immediately they quit their daily chores and prepared for the burial.

Undertakers and embalming were unknown in these mountain communities. Depending on whether a man or woman died, relatives of the same sex washed the body, dressed it in Sunday clothes, and laid it out on a plank or bed in a back room. In the meantime, one or two men would assemble a coffin. Some people stored a few pretty walnut boards in the barn loft for this purpose. Otherwise, pine, tulip poplar, or other suitable planks would be sawn at the local mill at no charge. While the carpenters worked, men and older boys converged at the cemetery with their shovels to help dig the grave. Women padded and lined the finished coffin with black cloth. By this time, neighbors would be bringing food for grieving relatives. A few

close friends kept a vigil with the family throughout the night.

The following morning, the coffin would be loaded into a wagon and driven slowly to the church. Most burials were made within twenty-four hours of the time the church bell tolled. After a lengthy service, community and family members filed past the coffin to say their goodbyes. After the men closed the grave, women circled round to decorate the fresh earth with flowers. I have been told that large-flowered trillium, a showy spring wildflower, was harvested so heavily for decorating graves during the Civil War that it nearly disappeared from some locales.

I have also spent hushed moments by gravesites in several of the pioneer cemeteries, trying to imagine what it was like for a mother to lose two or three of her children in one hard winter. During epidemics, community members might accomplish little else except making coffins and digging graves.

Not every gathering at the church yard was so somber. The last Sunday in May was Decoration Day, when everyone arrived for preaching and dinner on the grounds. Preparations might begin a week or so ahead with the men sprucing up the cemetery. Women baked pies and cakes, fried chickens, and cooked succulent roasts. They and the children made colorful paper flowers to place on the graves. If there was more than one church in the community, neighbors would meet at one, decorate, and go on to the next before finally serving the wonderful potluck meal.

Baptists were most numerous in mountain communities, followed by Methodists, and a few Presbyterians. Services were not held every Sunday since preachers tended several churches on alternate weekends. Sermons were long and serious, accompanied by traditional hymns sung a cappella. Although church was one of the few places community members could socialize, men sat on one side of the aisle during services and women on the other.

Mountain people tended to be deeply religious in the sense of traditional church doctrine. They also followed a number of "signs" interpreted from nature. Signs were based on the zodiac—a band of twelve constellations through which the paths of the sun, moon, and planets passed. Observers believed there was a relationship between these celestial bodies and the human body, thus each of the twelve signs represented a part

such as the head, heart, arms, or feet. Each was also assigned a quality, such as being barren or fruitful.

Rules for planting, butchering, cutting wood, and other tasks were based upon the phase of the moon and the positioning of planets within the zodiac. For instance, planting was best during days of the month when fruitful signs (Pisces, Scorpio, Taurus, or Cancer) dominate. Harvesting crops on a decreasing moon was said to make them keep better. Deadening trees to clear a field proved most successful if done in a barren sign.

Whether living by the signs actually increased harvests or made shingles lie flat is open to debate. Believers said the signs have their origin in the Biblical verse Ecclesiastes 3:1–2, "For everything there is a season, and a time for every matter under heaven: a time to be born, and a time to die; a time to plant, and a time to pluck up what is planted."

Surely a person aware enough of the natural world to watch the heavens and the signs knew when the soil was warm enough to plant, when danger of frost was past, or what kind of weather might have been in store for the next few days. Perhaps it was no coincidence that those who lived by the signs did have special insight into happenings of nature. Numerous residents of the southern Appalachians still follow the signs in modern gardening endeavors.

In the Smokies, it was commonly accepted that the winter would be bad if squirrels and hornets built their nests lower to the ground than usual. "When butterflies gather in bunches in the air," said one mountaineer, "winter is coming soon." "Three months after the first katydid begins hollerin'," another advised, "the first killing frost will come."

The settlers did not rely on radio or newspapers for their weather information. Rain was on the way if smoke dipped from the chimney to the ground, if the sun set with clouds around it, or there was a ring around the moon. All these observations indicate the approach of a low pressure system on today's weather maps—marked by falling barometric pressure (smoke drops) and increasing moisture (clouds around sun or moon).

The settlers watched for reactions of plants, animals, and inanimate objects to these changes and guessed accurately what weather was in store. The leaves of rosebay rhododendron tell temperature as reliably as a thermometer. At thirty-two degrees Fahrenheit, they droop and darken. If the air temperature falls to about twenty degrees, their edges roll inward. At zero, rosebay

Mountain people tended to be deeply religious. Gatherings at church were sometimes somber, as in the case of funerals, and sometimes happy occasions, such as annual Decoration Days.

leaves resemble tightly wrapped cigars. The view of the forest changes noticeably as a cold front moves in. Normally the large laurel leaves screen the understory. During cold spells, they coil so tightly that one can see past them much deeper into the woods.

The self-sufficient world of the mountaineer began to change in the late 1800s. Rich bottomland had already been claimed. As more people came into the region, they were forced farther up the hollows and onto steep mountain slopes. Few of these areas were free of rocks or level enough to allow large-scale farming. Those that tried found that when the sheltering trees were removed, drenching rains eroded the thin soil.

For many families, living on high slopes of the Great Smoky Mountains meant hard work with meager rewards. Their hardscrabble existence is reflected in place names such as Snag Mountain, Rocky Spur, Stony Gap, Scratch Britches, and Long Hungry Ridge.

Soon after white settlers came to the southern Appalachians, woodland bison and elk disappeared. In the 1800s, panthers and wolves met their demise. Hunting pressure severely reduced the numbers of deer, bear, grouse, and turkey.

Trees were cut locally to build cabins, to make furniture and tools, and to provide firewood, but prior to 1900, most logging in the Smokies was done on a small scale. A 1901 report to Congress described the southern Appalachians as having the "heaviest and most beautiful hard-wood forests of the continent."

That same year W. B. Townsend, owner of the Little River Lumber Company, began purchasing large tracts of Great Smokies land. Champion Coated Paper Company undertook a buying campaign that would eventually see it owning a fifth of the present park. While settlers cut selectively, snaking individual trees out of the woods with teams of oxen or mules, most lumber companies clear-cut all the marketable timber on a mountain tract. Cherry was valued for its scarcity, the beauty of its grain, and its regal mahogany tones that enrich with age. Tulip poplar accounted for the most profits because of its sheer volume. Huge oaks, hickories, ashes, basswoods, and magnolias also reached the mills.

Once sawyers cut a hillside, rail-mounted skidders moved into place. These cranelike machines reeled out as much as a mile of overhead cable, which was rigged

Settlers predicted the weather by observing plants and animals. In freezing weather, rhododendron leaves curl.

to a sturdy stump high on the mountain slope. Logs were attached to the cable in somewhat the way a ski lift works, and bellboys in the woods relayed signals to hoist away. It was a perilous job, especially if the cable snapped and logs came whizzing down the hillside. In places the skidder couldn't reach, workers known as "ballhooters" rolled logs downslope to a point where they could be retrieved.

Logging companies laid railroad track to boom towns such as Elkmont, Smokemont, Crestmont, Tremont, Proctor, and Ravens Fork. Gear-driven steam locomotives, powered by coal, pushed empty flatcars as far up the mountainsides as they could. At one time, track extended within a mile of Clingmans Dome, the highest point in the park. Steam-powered loaders piled the logs on the cars. The engineers backed the cog-driven engines down the steep grades, with brakemen manually setting the brakes on each car to prevent runaways. Conventional piston locomotives met the log cars at lower camps and hauled them to mills such as the one at Townsend. The narrow, winding road between Elkmont and Townsend is the original route of the Little River logging railroad.

The economy changed with the coming of the loggers. Some mountain landowners sold their marginal farmlands to the timber companies and moved away. Others took jobs as fellers, cable riggers, lumber stackers, surveyors, road builders, or blacksmiths. Still others marketed fresh eggs, apples, honey, and butter to men and women in the company towns. In addition to a flow of cash, boom towns brought electricity, movie theaters, hotels, and better roads to the mountains.

But at what price? Taking only large, straight boles, timber companies left huge piles of dying branches and treetops. Sparks from their equipment started disastrous fires that burned for months. With the trees and underbrush gone, soil eroded and fish disappeared from the muddy streams.

In a quarter of a century, sixty percent of the area now within Great Smoky Mountains National Park was cleared. Forests in the Little River, Big Creek, and Oconaluftee watersheds were denuded. The best timber was plucked from many other drainages. It was quite a spectacle while it lasted, with girths of the downed trees dwarfing the fellers and with railroads defying the mountain terrain. But within a few years the "most beautiful hard-wood forests of the continent" were nearly gone.

For a time, the words of Smokies native Horace Kephart, who decried the pillage of his beloved mountains, seemed to fall on deaf ears. Gradually he built support for a great eastern national park. Prior to the 1920s, most parks had been established on public lands in the West. On May 22, 1926, Congress authorized 6,600 private tracts to be incorporated into Great Smoky Mountains National Park, but the funds to purchase them had to come from state and private donations. The task was monumental, yet, working together, Tennessee and North Carolina raised $5 million, which was matched by philanthropist John D. Rockefeller. The 7,300 people living on 1,200 farms within the park were asked to relocate. Many sold willingly. Some, understandably, were reluctant to leave the only home they had ever known.

These were people who lived apart from mainstream America. For them, friends, family, and sense of place meant more than money. Life passed at a slower pace in these mountains. There was time for a mother to step back from stirring the steaming kettle of lye soap and dirty overalls, wipe her hands on her apron, adjust her long hair rolled into a tight bun, and gaze in awe at a hillside of dogwood trees in full bloom. There was time for a father to put down the harness he was mending and whittle a "gee-haw whammy-dittle" toy for his son. In the flickering evening glow of the kerosene lamp, there were moments when the whole family paused to listen to grandfather's rich baritone voice singing "Hand Me Down My Walking Cane" or reading verses from the Bible.

With the establishment of the park, a number of homes were torn down or allowed to decay. In places such as Oconaluftee, Cataloochee, Roaring Fork, and Cades Cove, however, a few remain. They speak to us of another era. If we pause there, we may feel the former owners' presences. Imagine the tinkle of the milk cow's bell as she walks to the barn on a foggy morning. In the gentle breeze of a fall afternoon, can we not hear the laughter of children filling their toesacks with chestnuts? As we breathe deeply of spring's rich, earthy scent, isn't that the distant "git up" of a plowman urging his mule to turn the winter-fallow garden?

The simple way of life has disappeared from the world with which most of us are familiar. In the Great Smoky Mountains, we can return to our roots for a time by listening to the voices that whisper from the woods.

Overleaf: *Life passed at a slower pace in the mountains. Relics of this former era remind us of a simpler lifestyle.*

MOUNTAIN HERITAGE

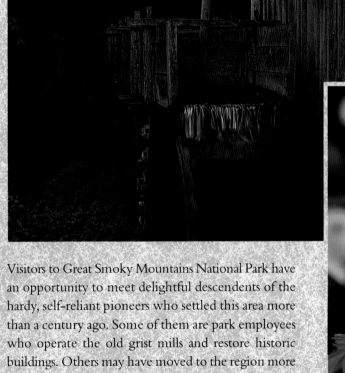

Visitors to Great Smoky Mountains National Park have an opportunity to meet delightful descendents of the hardy, self-reliant pioneers who settled this area more than a century ago. Some of them are park employees who operate the old grist mills and restore historic buildings. Others may have moved to the region more recently, but they give voice to the original mountaineers through "living history" demonstrations of traditional skills such as basketmaking, quilting, and food preservation.

At these sites, nature and history mingle. Deer graze beside cattle in the pastures, and fritillary butterflies sip nectar at favorite flowers in pioneer gardens. This blend reminds visitors that the special heritage preserved here includes people, plants, and wildlife.

For pioneers, autumn was a season of satisfaction. The woodshed would be stacked with firewood, and crisp apples would fill the root cellar. Cupboards would be lined with jars of fruits and vegetables. Neighbors worked together to shuck and shell corn or raise a new barn. Someone else's work, done while socializing, was never as dreary as doing your own tasks alone!

Now, as then, autumn is a time to celebrate this spirit of togetherness. Friends gather at Oconoluftee and Cades Cove on fall weekends to squeeze cane and boil the juice into sorghum molasses. The event is popular with park visitors, who not only have the chance to see "sweetnin'" made but can purchase a jar to take home with them.

Former residents also gather at Cades Cove in the spring and fall to reminisce and share old-time music. Hundreds of Smokies visitors join them. Friends sit under the shade trees, tapping their toes to fiddle tunes while munching on crusty chicken and fried pies from their picnic baskets. The bright sounds of a banjo, the steady, driving beat of guitars, and the booming notes of a stand-up bass accompany each fiddler. As you walk from one group of shade-tree musicians to the next, snippets of lyrics flood your ears, "down that long road again" . . . "little cabin in the hills of Caroline" . . . "the bright moon is shining on the valley, Mom and Dad are resting there today." In this place, the words seem most appropriate.

Russell Whitehead is the oldest resident of the cove present this particular Old-Timer's Day. At 102 years, he answers questions in a frail voice. Whenever someone asks to take his picture, though, he draws up proud in his chair. Russell says his family had a big garden. "We didn't see no bears or deer here—only up on Smoky," he recalls, gesturing over his shoulder to mountain peaks. His sister, Frances Brown, points to a clearing downstream from Cable mill. "We lived yonder, about as far as you can see."

A gray-haired man in Big Smith overalls pauses to show a horse-drawn hayrake to his grandson. Two similarly dressed men study the barn. "Don't see 'em with pine pole rafters like that anymore," one comments. "Now look at those boards," the other says, pointing to one section of the roof where the shingles overlap perfectly and another where they don't. "You can see those bowed-up ones was laid in the light of the moon."

Nearby, in a red calico dress and a sunbonnet she made herself, Audine Harmon tells a visitor about the house a few miles from here where she lived until she was fourteen. The cabin is gone, but three large trees mark the old homeplace. "Daddy had about a hundred hogs he turned loose in the woods," she explains. "They fattened on chestnuts, beechnuts, and acorns. We killed six hogs at Christmastime. We had a big garden and canned all our food. We had everything we needed."

NATURE'S DELICATE BALANCE

An important element in the lives of European settlers of the Great Smoky Mountains is gone from today's scene. At one time more than a third of the trees in the hardwood forests here were American chestnuts. Their broad crowns, covered with fragrant, cream-colored catkins, were a sight to behold each spring. The flowers developed into spiny-shelled burs that held large, sweet nuts. These nuts were relished by bears, deer, squirrels, chipmunks, turkeys, grouse, and mountaineers' free-ranging hogs.

Chestnuts were one of the settlers' few cash crops. Each autumn when breezes brought ripe nuts bumping through the limbs and plopping to the ground, families would go into the woods to collect them. A wagonload, when hauled on the two-day trip to Knoxville, would buy new shoes for all the children.

Unlike the oaks that have replaced them, chestnuts bloomed in June, after the threat of frost, and produced reliable mast crops each year. Oaks, whose early spring pollination can be disrupted by cold snaps, do not produce abundant acorns every year. For wildlife, as well as for the mountain people, the loss of the chestnut was a tragedy.

It is said that before the turn of the last century, an energetic squirrel could have traveled throughout the East without touching the ground by hopping among some 3.5 million chestnut trees. When Great Smoky Mountains National Park was dedicated in 1940, more than eighty-five percent of its chestnuts were dead or dying. What caused the massive decline? The culprits were a few unnoticed fungal spores on the seedlings of imported Oriental chestnut trees.

Asian chestnuts are resistant to the spores of the chestnut fungus. Once in the United States, however, spores spread quickly on the wind from imported to native trees. Cankers with orange bumps protruding from them were discovered on the bark of chestnut trees in New York City in 1904. By 1930, trees within four-fifths of the chestnut's range were ailing. Once under the bark, fungal spores spread out in a fan-shaped growth that disrupts the flow of nutrients, strangling the tree.

The former abundance of chestnut trees is reflected in Smokies place-names: Upper and Lower Chestnut Flats, Big and Little Chestnut Ridges, Chestnut Cove, Chestnut Branch, and Chestnut Top. Go to any of these places today and look in the understory for clusters of silver-hued dead branches around an old stump. Among them you will likely find some live sprouts with coarsely toothed, elongated oval leaves. Although the blight killed standing trees older than about ten years, root systems of many chestnuts remained alive. They continue to produce viable scions.

Several rays of hope glimmer for these surviving chestnut trees. Blight infected European chestnuts in 1917, but in Italy the trees developed a resistance to the blight. Scientists in the United States are working with remaining American chestnut trees that are infected but have not died, searching for a similar blight-weakening agent.

Other researchers are trying to hybridize American chestnuts with disease-resistant Chinese chestnuts.

Although a blight killed mature chestnut trees half a century ago, viable scions continue to sprout from the roots of these hardy plants.

Relished by a variety of wildlife, chestnuts also were used as a cash crop by the mountaineers.

Oriental trees are short and squatty. Among the desirable qualities of the American chestnut are its tall stature and broad crown. In order to combine the form of the American chestnut with the blight-resistance of the Oriental, crossbreeding must take place.

Beginning in 1987, scions were collected from chestnuts still sprouting in the park. They were grafted to healthy chestnut roots at the University of Tennessee. Five generations of seed will be hybridized. Resulting offspring should have ninety-five percent the height and stature of American chestnuts, plus disease resistance from their Chinese heritage. It is hoped this fifth generation seed will be ready to plant shortly into the twenty-first century. Perhaps genetic engineering undreamed of a hundred years ago will return the American chestnut to its rightful place in eastern forests.

Since many of the trees in the Smokies are similar to those of Europe and Asia, diseases from abroad find favorable growing conditions in the southern Appalachians. Agents that attack Fraser fir, elm, moun-

tain ash, dogwood, and butternut trees are already established in the park. Gypsy moths, which defoliate oaks, and insects that prey on hemlock trees have been discovered elsewhere in the East. They could spread to the Smokies within the next few years.

Dogwood anthracnose, a fungus believed to be from Asia, was discovered in New York and Washington in 1978. It has spread rapidly to native dogwoods, much as the chestnut blight attacked chestnut trees. The disease was confirmed in the Smokies in 1988. Dogwoods that grow in moist hollows, where their leaves stay damp and air circulation is poor, seem more prone to dieback than trees in warmer, drier locations. Unless effective countermeasures are discovered soon, widespread vistas of white dogwood flowers against a backdrop of emerging spring green foliage may, like chestnut forests, be limited to fond memories.

In 1963 an invading insect was found in the northeastern part of the park. Since then, ninety-five percent of the Fraser firs in the Great Smokies have been decimated by the balsam woolly adelgid. A century ago, adelgids hitched a ride from Europe to the United States on nursery stock. They are half as large as a pinhead and wingless, but so light they are blown from tree to tree. Adelgids hide under the bark and insert their tubelike mouths into the cambium. While sucking nutrients from fir sap, the adelgid's saliva reacts with the cells around its mouth, causing them to grow abnormally and disrupting the flow of moisture from the roots up to the crown.

Adelgids reproduce abundantly. Each female lays about a hundred eggs that hatch into "crawlers." Crawlers disseminate to other portions of that tree, or to a new tree, attaching and drinking sap. They mature quickly and lay more eggs, repeating the cycle numerous times. By the end of a year, the offspring of one adelgid can produce three million new insects. Adelgids cover themselves in woolly white wax for protection. Although a single insect would be difficult to see without a magnifying glass, infected trees are noticeable by the patchy, whitewashed appearance of the bark where a mass infection occurs.

Mature Fraser firs can die within three years of the initial adelgid attack. Whole forests now stand bare in the Smokies. Although the process is labor-intensive, park resource managers presently treat the Fraser firs along the Clingmans Dome and Balsam Mountain roads by spraying them with a special soap that dissolves the insects' protective coating. Adelgids die from exposure, while the soap breaks down rapidly without harmful side-effects. Unfortunately, this is not a permanent solution to the adelgid problem, but it is keeping a few thousand Fraser fir trees alive until better control measures are found.

Red spruce, the other dominant conifer in the park's highest forests, may also be in trouble. Core samples show that since the 1950s at the highest elevations, spruce trees have grown very little. Deterioration has accelerated in the past few years. Some spruce needles have developed brown spots; needles have dropped from other trees. About ninety percent of the park's red spruces were healthy in 1985. Four years later, only fifty percent were still as vigorous.

The Environmental Protection Agency has established a sophisticated sampling station in a spruce-fir forest on Mount Mitchell, fifty miles northeast of the park. Like Clingmans Dome and other Smokies peaks with sensitive boreal forests, Mount Mitchell is bathed in clouds on three days of every four. Equipment on Mount Mitchell monitors airborne pollution. It has recorded compounds including ozone, nitrogen oxide, and sulfur dioxide swirling around in the fog and mist. On some days, the atmospheric moisture drops to a pH level of 2.3 (pH 7 is neutral). The effect is comparable to sprinkling lemon juice instead of tapwater on your houseplants.

Scientists theorize that increasing amounts of ozone in the atmosphere cause the tiny gas exchange pores in leaves to remain open longer than normal. While the pores are open, acid mists leach nutrients from the plant. Higher-than-normal levels of nitrogen in the pollution may overfertilize the trees, causing stress. Acids also enter the soil with rain and snow. They remove important trace minerals such as calcium and magnesium. In the process, they release aluminum compounds that are drawn in through the roots. Aluminum is toxic to root hairs, killing plants' vital water- and nutrient-absorbing organs.

Figuring out exactly what pollutant manifests what reaction in a particular plant is akin to trying to find the way out of a complex maze. In all likelihood, the combination of many pollutants is more damaging that the presence of just one or two types. Scientists do know that the highest levels of tree death and defoliation occur on windward slopes, areas exposed to the most severe pollution. Pollution seems to weaken trees so other insects or diseases can take hold. Woolly adelgids, for example, are more concentrated on fir trees on exposed slopes.

Scientists also know that similar signs of forest decline were noted in Germany, Switzerland, and Scandinavia several decades ago. As in the United States, European studies link forest declines to airborne pollution. Factories, refineries, power plants, and autos worldwide belch pollutants into the air. The toxics can be carried for hundreds of miles on upper-level wind currents. They freely cross state and international boundaries, coming to rest over cities, on mountaintops, or in lakes far from the source. During the winter, north winds push pollutants from the high-sulfur coal burned in the midwestern cities of Detroit, Dayton, and Cincinnati over the Smokies. In the summer, much of the gray haze here originates in the steel belt around Birmingham, Alabama, arriving on prevailing southwesterly winds.

The high altitude forest decline in the Great Smokies

Overleaf: *Dogwood anthracnose, a recently introduced disease, is spreading among flowering dogwood trees. (Photo © by Pat Toops)*

Since 1963, 95 percent of the Fraser firs in the park have been killed by balsam woolly adelgids. These tiny insects hide under loose bark and suck nutrients from fir sap.

Airborne pollutants are contained in the fog that swirls around mountain peaks. This pollution may be weakening or killing certain trees. In the Great Smokies, scientists are trying to determine the extent of the problem by exposing native plants to varying levels of ozone.

Spring displays of white dogwood flowers may be in jeopardy.

Wild hogs will uproot spring beauties and other plants with fleshy roots to satisfy their voracious appetites.

is significant cause for alarm. Already major portions of the world's only Fraser fir forest have been decimated. Shrubby blackberries and fire cherries are invading the sunny openings where firs once grew. Specialized mosses, lichens, insects, and animal inhabitants of these forests are at risk.

It is unrealistic to think we can eliminate all pollution, since pollutants are by-products of economic success. But we should not shrug off pollution as someone else's problem. Each of us must strive to reduce detrimental aspects in whatever ways we can.

Even when we have the best intentions, human interference with the natural scheme sometimes upsets nature's delicate balance. Such was introduction of the European wild boar early in the twentieth century. About sixty of these creatures escaped from a North Carolina hunting preserve and fled to the surrounding woods. There they interbred with farmers' free-ranging pigs. While settlers still inhabited the park, the pigs were hunted and eaten. Afterward, hogs increased unchecked.

Old World pigs are wily, adaptable creatures. Although they weigh up to 150 pounds, they are quick and quiet in the woods. Large at the shoulder, tapering to slim hips, with a tufted, turned-up tail, wild boars run or swim to escape. If cornered, they use sharp tusks to defend themselves against bears, dogs, or humans.

Wild hogs use their tusks like the tines of a rototiller, churning the soil in search of tuberous roots, nuts, acorns, mushrooms, and snails. They also devour salamanders, rodents, snakes, the eggs of ground-nesting birds and reptiles, and a variety of ferns, grasses, and wildflowers. One adult hog during the fall and winter can consume more than half a ton of acorns, at the expense of native turkeys, grouse, deer, bears, and squirrels. Hogs can decimate whole stands of flowers as common as spring beauties or as rare as orchids. They can turn pristine creeks into foul-smelling wallows.

Without control, animals that have eight to twelve piglets per litter and bear one or two litters per year will overrun the park. Yet regional hunters covet free-ranging wild hogs for meat and as exciting quarry for trophies. After several years of controversy, an agreement allows park rangers to shoot offending hogs in remote backcountry areas. Nearer roads, however, the hogs are trapped and relocated to forests in Tennessee and North Carolina where they can be hunted. Reports

of damage have declined since hog control began in 1986. Although the pigs may never be eliminated, monitoring will keep them at levels low enough to protect the park's diverse flora and fauna.

Another primer on nature's balance in the Great Smokies is the reintroduction of the red wolf. Red wolves are shy, nocturnal predators, larger than coyotes but smaller than gray wolves. They originally ranged from the Atlantic coast and the Ohio River to Texas. Both red and gray wolves formerly roamed the Smoky Mountains.

In 1970, the remaining wild red wolves were captured by the U. S. Fish and Wildlife Service and placed in a breeding program. At that time, red wolves had been reduced by bounty hunting, habitat loss, and interbreeding with coyotes to a very small population in coastal Louisiana. Captive wolves have now increased to more than a hundred animals. Within the past few years some have been reintroduced to isolated refuges and barrier islands in the southeastern United States, where they are once more rearing pups in the wild.

It is from this stock that two pairs of adult red wolves were brought to the Smokies in January 1991. According to chief of resources management Joe Abrell, "Great Smoky Mountains National Park is one of the largest and wildest areas left within the red wolf's historic range." The goal, Abrell explained, is to eventually build a viable population of fifty to seventy-five wolves in the park.

The adult wolves were allowed to acclimatize and bear pups in a large, secluded pen. Keepers supplied food typical of what the wolves find on their own—primarily rodents, raccoons, rabbits, and wild hogs. Red wolves do not hunt in packs as gray wolves do, thus they prey on smaller animals. The first wolves were released in autumn 1991. If their reintroduction is successful, four or five more pairs will be freed in the Smokies in 1992. It is expected that each family will establish a range of eighty to a hundred square miles. The wolves will be fitted with radio transmitters and tracked carefully. Should they wander outside the park, they will be captured and returned.

The greatest uncertainty about the reintroduction is how red wolves will interact with coyotes. Coyotes were primarily a western mammal, but with extermination of wolves in the East, they have expanded their range. They first entered the Smokies in the 1980s. The

Red wolves are being reintroduced to the Great Smoky Mountains under carefully controlled conditions. (Photo © Ken L. Jenkins, courtesy Great Smoky Mountains National Park)

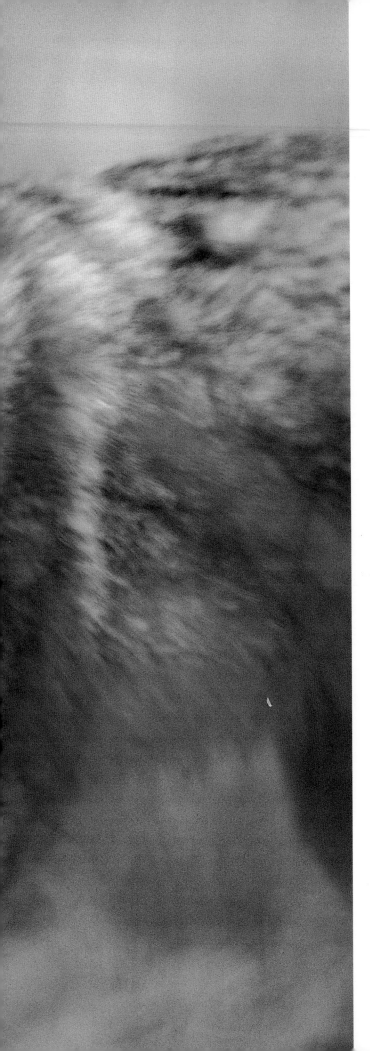

coyote population here is small, and it is hoped red wolves will eventually replace them.

Coyotes are successful survivors, however. They eat a variety of prey and are able to endure by stalking mice if no other food is available. Eastern coyotes are up to ten pounds heavier than their western counterparts, perhaps a result of interbreeding with red wolves or domestic dogs. Coyotes compete well on the fringes of urban areas. In the wild, they commonly drive smaller red foxes from their territories.

Mention of wolves once stirred deep emotions of fear and hatred in the hearts of pioneer families. Now our perspective is more balanced. We understand that wolves are top predators in nature's food chain and we respect them for being hardy, cunning creatures. In the Great Smokies, we have a unique opportunity to watch red wolves, coyotes, and red foxes strive for a balance. Will this wilderness reaccommodate the wolves? Will coyotes, the newcomers, be squeezed out? If so, will red foxes prosper? Being able to study predator versus predator in this process of adaptation will provide a fascinating opportunity.

In the absence of wolves, coyotes have moved into the park from the west. If red wolves reestablish themselves, will they displace the invading coyotes? (Photo © by Maslowski Wildlife Productions)

SPLENDORS OF THE SEASONS

Great Smoky Mountains National Park, at once remote and wild yet open to millions of people, is a place of refuge. For its animal inhabitants, the park is a haven from hunting and habitat destruction. For human visitors, this is an arena in which to see nature taking a basically unaltered course. Within this eastern wilderness, we encounter cycles of life and death and witness the splendors of the seasons.

Who can say which season is more spectacular? Each has its own charms. Perhaps spring is most welcome, for this is a time when beauty bursts from underground bulbs and tightly rolled buds. The dreariness of gray skies and snowflakes is replaced with flurries of serviceberry petals and delicate bloodroot blossoms. A sense of rebirth wells up as lingering rays of sunlight warm the mountains.

The first signs of new life are buds swelling on the trees. You notice them most at sunrise and sunset—knobby latticework silhouetted against a stark orange glow. As the buds reveal their contents, woodlands blush with the delicate rouges of maple and basswood and glow with golden hues of hobblebush and hickory.

If you visit the woods as the light of dawn sifts through the misty trees, you may catch a glimpse of a chicken-sized bird walking cautiously across the forest floor. At first you may think it is a puff of wind rustling the fallen leaves, for the ruffed grouse wears woodland hues of russet, umber, and sepia. But you will see the gleam in its eye when it hops onto a mossy log and peers alertly in all directions. Balancing on tiptoe, the grouse fluffs its feathers, drops its wings, and fans them

to the front of its breast. Each wingbeat comes faster and louder than the last. *Putt . . . putt . . . putt . . . brrummm*. Black ruffs on the grouse's neck flair to frame its small head.

The grouse takes a few quick steps down the log, shakes his ruff, and drums again. Then, as if materialized from leafy camouflage, a hen appears. The cock fluffs his finery and hops down from the log to stand beside her. He displays again, sounding like an old tractor wheezing to life. She picks coquettishly at the moss. Once more he thumps and whirs, carrying out a ritual that has continued for uncounted centuries.

In the dank earth under winter's blanket of leaves, spotted salamanders arouse. Lured by an unexplained signal, they emerge on a rainy night and trek overland to a breeding pond. The males, which live twenty to thirty years, come annually. Females make the journey every other year. They follow traditional routes, navigating by familiar odors or landmarks.

Upon arrival, females secrete pheromones through their moist skin. Enraptured males gather in writhing masses on the bottom of the pond, bumping the females with their noses. The dance stimulates males to deposit tiny, mushroom-shaped clusters of sperm near females. During the next several nights, each female randomly picks up with her cloaca ten to twenty spermatophores and internalizes them to fertilize her eggs. Reproduction takes place without copulation.

Within a few days, the eight-inch females attach fist-sized clusters of jellied eggs to underwater sticks and vegetation. Eggs hatch into gilled juveniles in about

The spring forest awakens with tender green foliage and snow-white dogwood blossoms.

Burnished rays of the morning sun thread through the woods, spotlighting a trout lily.

Gaze in the direction of the dawn, and all you will see are silhouettes of ridge upon rolling ridge.

A garden spider's web is adorned with dewy highlights.

a month. In another month or two, young salamanders leave the water for the woodlands. They will return to this pond as adults.

Summer arrives without fanfare. In May the nights can still be frosty on the mountaintops, where wildflowers bloom in profusion. On the valley floors, the air is already sultry. Morning fogs fill the hollows. Afternoon haze obscures distant vistas. Clouds drift lazily among the peaks, dropping a little moisture, then breaking into cottony puffs with sunbeams penetrating them. The forests are lush and green, dripping from recent thundershowers.

This is a season of abundance, a time when red-eyed vireos can find all the caterpillars they need to satisfy a nest of hungry chicks. It is a time when sleek deer graze contentedly among the belly-high grasses in meadows at Cades Cove and Cataloochee. Cicadas drone from the treetops. Rhododendrons paint the hills and streambanks in pastel shades. Deep within the forest,

gaudy orange and black beetles tiptoe on mossy logs, emitting sweet-pungent scents that signal mates to join them. Lacy ferns are adorned with dewy highlights that sparkle like stars in the night sky.

Summer slips away as stealthily as it arrived, leaving first from the mountaintops, but lingering another month or so in the verdant hollows. The first hint of autumn's approach is a display of red and yellow witchhobble leaves. By mid-September at higher elevations, pin cherry, mountain ash, and birch achieve their most brilliant colors of the season. In the lower forests, individual dogwoods, sumacs, gums, sourwoods, and Virginia creeper vines are firebrands among a sea of green.

Summer's misty haze has disappeared from skies that are now intensely blue. Ravens dip and roll on the freshening breezes. The sun's warmth is welcome, counteracting long, cool shadows. This is a mellow season, when the songs of autumn linger in my mind.

Overleaf: *Summer air in the valleys is still and sultry. Morning fog fills the hollows.*

Pastel rosebay rhododendron flowers paint the banks of Laurel Falls.

Above: *In whimsical masquerade, a well-camouflaged wood frog sits quietly in the fallen leaves. (Photo © by Harry Ellis.)* **Right:** *Individual red maples are firebrands among a sea of green.*

The winter forest is quiet except for the chirps of finches, juncos, or an occasional chickadee.

Along streams in winter, overhanging branches are outlined in filigrees of ice.

At this time of year, crickets chirp with a deliberateness not heard in summer's rush. Along the streams, hummingbirds buzz among the bright red cardinal flowers. Small blue butterflies flit from lobelias to asters and ageratums, lazily sipping nectar. On the hillsides, the colorful leaves are highlighted by brilliant shafts of sunlight.

For connoisseurs of fall color, the hue of each tree is a recognizable signature. The canary yellow of goosefoot maple, the glowing scarlet of gum, the crimson of sourwood, the gold of beech, and the saffron of hickory all serve to identify them from a distance as surely as do leaf shapes. To my way of thinking, there is no more impressive sight than an autumn hardwood forest dominated by sugar maples. Walking beneath these trees at this season, it is as if golden light streams in through resplendent stained-glass windows. The spectacle is a fleeting one, however, as each breath of wind brings a gentle shower of leaves raining down to the forest floor. Within a few days, the dazzle of autumn is transformed into muted tones of winter.

Winter sees many of the smaller woodland creatures—frogs and salamanders, turtles, insects, and snakes—snuggled beneath a coverlet of leaf litter. The forest is silent, save for the quiet chirps of juncos feeding on the ground or an occasional *chickadee-dee-dee* call overhead.

With all but a few wrinkled beech and oak leaves gone from the limbs, bark and branch patterns are the best way to identify trees now. Sycamore is easy—a streamside giant with ashy-white bark. Silverbell trunks are pocked and knotted with lumpy burls. The buttonlike buds of dogwood, arranged on twigs that diverge in twos, stand out in bold relief when covered by frost or a dusting of snow.

Prolonged snowfall is unusual at the park's lower elevations, but ice storms are common in winter. Tree branches shine with a blinding silvery glaze when the sun finally emerges from storm clouds. At higher elevations, midstream rocks and overhanging branches are skirted with frozen filigrees of ice. Waterfalls look like sugar frosting running down the sides of a cake; icicle daggers dangle from bluff faces. Sometimes fog freezes on the trees, creating fragile, sparkling crystals clinging like snowy lace to the branches. In the ephemeral moments before the delicacies melt, they are sometimes haloed by sunlight, creating a mesmerizing fairyland of shimmering white.

Each season in the Smokies speaks with its own eloquent voice. Whether the mountains are mantled in their finest hues of autumn or blanketed in white, they beckon us to explore. From rocks that are among the oldest in the country to fresh spring blossoms on the hillsides, there is a sense of continuity here.

On the mountaintops you can see colors and patterns that reveal balds and boreal forests. You can gaze at hollows draped in verdant hardwood forests and imagine the pristine streams gurgling through them. You can watch distant valleys disappear into the smoky blue haze.

There is always something that lures me back, much as my eyes are drawn repeatedly to the varied and colorful scraps in a mountaineer's patchwork quilt. These are serene, yet exhilarating, vistas. They offer telling glimpses, almost as if the quilt patches have come together to reveal age-old secrets of the mountains. These views speak of a land at once rugged and fragile. They praise the preservation of a rich cultural and biological heritage all too rare in our modern lives.

Among my favorite memories of Smoky Mountain vistas are mornings spent alone on Clingmans Dome, watching the sunrise from this highest point in the park. Gaze with me in the direction of Cataloochee Balsam, where the warm promise of the dawn glows. All you will see are silhouettes of ridge upon rolling ridge. Turn your back on that scene and squint far to the west, past Chestnut Ridge and Cold Spring Knob, to Gregory Bald and Rich Mountain if the mists allow. No twinkling lights save for the fading morning star. No roads. No sound except for the hoarse croak of the raven. Here you can sense the vastness of the Great Smokies. Here you will realize that these mountains have remained secluded in many ways from the sea of change that surrounds them.

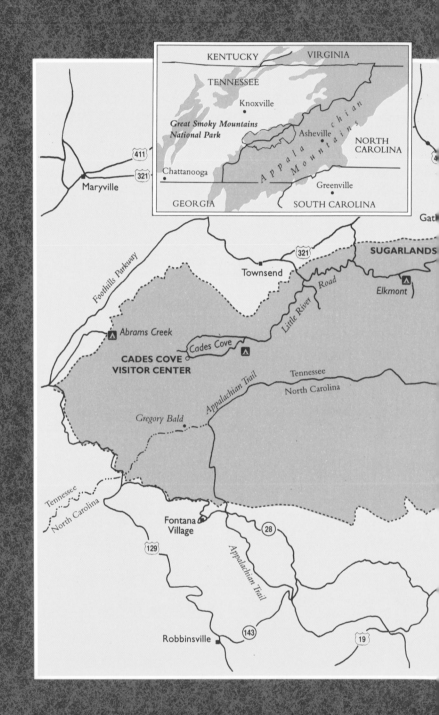